THE
Dried Flower
Garden

A fireplace arrangement makes a stunning focus point in a large living room. Carlina acaulis, *bamboo, gypsophila, leeks, peach helichrysum and glycerined beech are placed in a large wicker basket on the grate.*

THE

Dried Flower Garden

ANN LINDSAY MITCHELL

*Arrangements by Yvonne Mallett,
illustrations by Chris Silver
and photography by Derick Bonsall*

B.T. BATSFORD LTD, LONDON

First published 1990
© Ann Lindsay Mitchell 1990

ISBN 0 7134 6221 3

Illustrations by Chris Silver
Photographs by Derick Bonsall

Filmset by Latimer Trend & Company Ltd, Plymouth
Printed and bound in Hong Kong

for the publishers
B.T. Batsford Ltd,
4 Fitzhardinge Street,
London W1H 0AH

Contents

ACKNOWLEDGEMENTS

With many thanks to:

Bettina, Lady Thompson, Shelagh Ross, and Pat Gibb of Priorwood Gardens, the National Trust for Scotland's garden in Melrose. Part of this garden is devoted totally to growing flowers, shrubs, and herbs for drying.

Louise Carstairs of Everlastings; Scottish Dried Flowers, Carnbee, Fife, whose dried flower business must surely produce the most colourful array of flowers possible.

Dr Gordon Smith of the Department of Plant Science at the University of Aberdeen for all his help, and donation of plants.

The Countess of Crawford, who gave advice and allowed me to raid her wonderful garden for examples to illustrate; also to Donald Lamb, the gardener at her home at Balcarres Castle in Fife, which is opened once a year through the Scotland's Gardens Scheme.

The following who allowed me to gather material from their gardens for the illustrations in this book: Mrs A. Duff; Elspeth Dunbar; Ba Hare Duke; Sheila Lendrum; my mother, Mary Lindsay; Julia Logan; Morna Miller of the Cottage Gallery, Newtyle, where many of the photos were taken; Ann Rodgie; Dr Smith; Diane Smythe, and Sheila Wood.

The road verges and nature reserves cared for by Fife, Tayside and Grampian regional councils, as well as the highlands and islands, from where many of the wild plants were carefully picked.

Yvonne Mallet, especially, who supplied the flower arrangements, many flowers, advice, enthusiasm, talent, and inspiration.

My husband, Alexander, and sons, Robert, Duncan and Haldane, who have put up with flowers instead of food on the kitchen table.

A white hallway sets off the delicate blues and pinks of this arrangement and a white porcelain basket makes an attractive container. Peach helichrysum, peach statice, hydrangea, bamboo and Achillea ptarmica.

INTRODUCTION

Not many years ago, my father was visiting us and wandered down the length of our not inconsiderable garden to observe me at work. Keeping a safe distance from the chemical warfare I appeared to be waging amid the endless rows of summer vegetables, he gazed in silence for a while. I was rather proud of the beanfeast I supplied for the less than enthusiastic family all summer long, and boasted a little.

'You know', he observed, 'it's winter you really want to grow for. In the summer, fruit and veg are cheap and plentiful, but that time between December and June . . . now that is the time to plan for.'

It's exactly the same with flowers, I think. All summer long there is a delectable surfeit, and then all too abruptly it is over. Flowers in winter seem a real winner in tricking nature. I've dropped many habits over the years, using chemical warfare in the garden and growing multitudes of beans being two of them. Now I plan for the winter, and it is doubly rewarding.

Drying flowers is fairly inexpensive. They can be given away as presents (the cheapest presents to post I know, apart from a cheque), for fund-raising events, and can transform your home.

Nothing boosts morale better than gazing into the midst of a bunch of brilliant helichrysums in late January – except perhaps a sunbed or a ticket to the Caribbean. But they do require effort and a little know-how. Even seasoned gardeners baulk at the idea of which plants to grow, when to pick, how to dry, where to dry them, how to store them, and then, finally how to arrange them. Where on earth do you start?

Well, before you sink your hands into the earth, read the beginning chapters in this book, and the whole subject should become clearer. These first chapters are essential reading.

The middle chapters, on the actual plants to grow, can be dipped into and items picked up from time to time, rather like a cookery book. The plants are listed in alphabetical order under Latin names, and common names are given in brackets.

The end chapters are an easy beginners' guide to what to do with them when you have grown, picked, hung, pressed, and dried them.

If you have a large garden, a small one, a patio, or just some pot plants, you can still make use of much of the information in this book.

Square basket filled with Fagus sylvatica *'Cuprea' (copper beech), yellowy green* Alchemilla mollis *(lady's mantle), hydrangea heads sprayed with green, linum seedheads (flax), and bright orange* Physalis alkekengi *(Chinese lanterns).*

Drying

FLOWERS

Keep uppermost in your mind the word 'quantity' when the idea of drying flowers is about to become a reality; imagine drying in armfuls rather than small bunches. By the very act of drying, many leaves, flowers, and seedheads may shrink by around 50 per cent. This does not mean that you have to find an armful rather than a bunch every time you hang something up to dry, but it does mean that you should dry much, much more than you ever think you may possibly use. You certainly will!

For many people, the attraction of dried flowers in shop windows is that their generous profusion looks so temptingly lush, bountiful, and extravagant. It is often disappointing, therefore, as you may well have discovered, to buy one pretty bunch, take it home, and try to arrange the flowers. Many people try to spread this one small bouquet around, striving to make it look as generous as possible by popping the odd half dozen flowers into at least a couple of containers. This is a mistake, and hints on how to arrange are detailed later in this book. The main point is, though, that one small bunch ends up looking quite lost, unless you add to it yourself with greenery, seedheads, and even weeds.

Dried flowers can be expensive, because they are both labour-intensive and prey to unseasonal wet, windy growing seasons. These high prices are a great incentive for growing and drying your own flowers; unless you have a great deal of money to spare you will never achieve the

beautiful image of great baskets and jugs of flowers, unless you grow them yourself.

So how do you launch yourself into drying in quantity?

An easy first step is to pad out the shop-bought blooms with as much dried greenery as possible, and if you can't dry many flowers because you have no garden or time, then gathering greenery and drying as much as possible (many weeds dry well) is a large first step. You will undoubtedly use it all.

In this book are listed over 130 different plants from which you can easily dry the flowers, leaves, or seedheads, or sometimes all three. Also included are herbs, which, while obviously not being dried flowers, will provide an interesting scent for at least the first month or so.

11

FOR THOSE WITH A GARDEN

If you have a garden, then you can grow as many of these plants listed in the book as you like. The majority can be grown in any soil, and under most climatic conditions. Within your garden there may already be many species which you were unaware could be dried; or perhaps you did not realize that some are so easy to grow, or from where to obtain the seeds. All this information is contained within this book.

Be encouraged to grow plenty, and attempt to dry as much material as you can. Look around also for material which you do not have, or which you have not enough room to grow. Read on for ideas on how to increase your stock for drying.

FOR THOSE WITHOUT A GARDEN

If you do not have a garden, but have perhaps a patio or terrace, try growing some of the annuals as pot plants, and try also pinching leaves for drying from, for example, coleus or ferns, and pressing them. Few prolific pot plants miss the odd leaf. Pot-grown hydrangeas and *Dianthus caryophyllus* can provide a couple of blooms. Alliums, *Acanthus mollis*, and celosias can be grown very well in outdoor pots.

Alternatively, you can buy flowers from a florist specifically in order to dry them. For example, bunches of gypsophila, or herbs, can often be bought at the end of a Saturday for reduced prices.

Check through this book for what plants and flowers will dry, and then you may be in a position to snap up bargains.

If all this effort to gather armfuls of material to dry is still beginning to sound rather expensive and extravagant, and you can neither grow your own, nor afford to buy flowers specifically for drying, then look around for free flowers.

The simplest way might be to ask friends with large gardens (or larger than yours anyway) to spare a few for you. You can always return a dried assorted bunch one day as a present. Also, keep your eyes open for any garden or public park that has a professional gardener wandering around inside it. Most likely places are the public parks which contain flower beds, although many leaves, branches, and seedheads of weeds can be dried as well. Gardeners are usually the most generous of people, only too willing to give away samples of their care to anyone who shows interest: 'that freemasonry of gardeners' as Vita Sackville-West described it.

Other possible sources in Britain are National Trust gardens, gardens that are open under charitable schemes once or twice a year, or plant-growing nurseries. By offering a donation to the charity scheme supported by a particular garden, you might well be fortunate.

Most professional gardeners, and here I include anyone who is being paid for lifting a fork, are a jump ahead of us amateurs. Herbaceous borders are quite properly chopped down and tidied up before they are past their best, unlike my own, since I cannot bear to cut down anything until the last flower has vanished. If you keep an eye firmly

attuned to the cycle of the gardening year, you could, for example, negotiate a bunch of delphiniums, *Stachys lanata* or aconitum still in reasonable enough heart to dry.

Making friends with gardeners in public parks might reap rich pickings. Most gardeners are very willing to discuss any aspect of their work, and would welcome anyone who asks them for a bunch or so from their domain, but don't appreciate people who help themselves.

If you can persuade someone to let you have some prunings to take home, you will probably have to be willing to go along and collect them as soon as they are chopped down, or very soon afterwards. Not only will they want to dispose of rubbish as fast as possible, but your precious flower heads will quickly be damaged after lying in a wheelbarrow for a few hours.

Roses are well worth considering. Most parks grow hybrid teas and floribundas, many of which can be dried. When roses

are pruned in the autumn they are still usually producing buds, and it is buds that can best be dried. The most tactful way to accept a gift of rose prunings is to welcome the lot, take home the entire barrow load, and sort them out. And, since rose prunings are usually burnt, you are not depriving next year's blooms of sustenance.

(Check for details about drying roses under 'Rosa' page 81.)

Consult this book for plants which produce material which can be dried, then look out for those plants in other gardens or parks.

FINDING MORE MATERIAL FOR NOTHING

In an effort to bulk out your collection of material for drying, do not ignore flowers, leaves and seedheads from the wild. While not wishing to encourage anyone to rip up rare plants, there is a wealth of material growing not only in the countryside, but on road verges, riversides, and derelict ground, which can be dried beautifully. No item suggested in this book is an endangered species, but, even so, always make sure that you never pick the only flower or seedhead of that type, and never pull anything up by the roots. Read the section on vegetables and herbs (wild), page 82, and start searching.

GREENERY

Most people will be surprised by the amount of greenery which I recommend for drying. Why, apart from the fact that most of it is plenteous and encouragingly free, does one need to dry and preserve so much that remains green?

My offer, once, to arrange the flowers in our local church (so cold in this northern spot that the water usually freezes in the vase for the winter months) with the suggestion that I should bring a posy of dried flowers was politely declined. The lady in question assured me that she did not care greatly for dried flowers and never had, despite her obvious and extensive knowledge of gardening and flowers.

However, a couple of weeks and several feet of snow later, she must have concluded that this was not such a bad notion after all, as a narrow-necked embossed brass pitcher had been filled with a rigidly symmetrical array of teasels, bullrushes and honesty seedpods. My three-year-old son had to be restrained from using one as a sword! Once installed, the flowers stayed and stayed, I recall, for weeks.

A month later, I realized that what was predominantly wrong with this arrangement was its sterility, which arose from the lack of any form of green – the symbol of growth.

You can judge this for yourself. Buy or pick a small bunch of flowers, dried and devoid of green. Then surround them with a few ferns, for example; the difference is magical. Another bonus in having plenty of leaves around a bunch of flowers is that, not only do they make a smallish posy go a lot further, but they make life much easier when you are trying to concoct an effective basketful.

This is not to say that all dried arrangements will always need green. Stunning things can be done without a trace of greenery, as can be clearly seen in the photographs in this book. It is just that greenery is essential to complement many dried flowers, and somehow produces arrangements that, in the long term, are softer on the eye.

Most of the selection listed in this book can be successfully dried by pressing. A few can be hung-dried. Once again, think in

15

bulk, and press or hang as much as you can. You will undoubtedly use it all.

What appeals to me most is the rather confident throw-away English country-house look of a bundle of sweet-smelling blooms, freshly gathered while wandering up the garden path, and lowered promptly into an informal container. To achieve this confident look I finally found that it is best to treat dried flowers in exactly the same way as fresh ones, and to pick and select leaves to surround the flowers and mingle with them. Not only are lots of leaves, even when still stiff from being pressed, perfect for bulking out not too many flowers, they are also adept at hiding bare stems or wire.

You can never have enough greenery. It is amazing how even a tiny bunch of flowers surrounded by leaves looks passable as a present. Even if you have masses left over – I once pressed a forest of ferns under the spare room carpet, which came into their own as a complete arrangement for a little-used fireplace – you will find a use for them, and be thankful for their presence.

It is, perhaps, rather ironic that even the most splendid dried flowers rarely look effective

without greenery, but you can always produce something wonderful with greenery alone.

While dried greenery will happily disguise stalks, so it will cover up foam, or the broken corner of a once pretty box that has been pressed into service as a container.

DRYING METHODS

PICKING AND PREPARING FOR DRYING

The golden rule is to pick a little every day, if you are collecting material from your garden. This way it takes a few minutes of your time, seems effortless, yet the material will mount up very quickly.

Try to hang, prop upright, or press as soon as you pick, or at least on the same day. If you cannot, then stand your flowers in cold water in a cool place.

Each plant listed in this book has instructions on exactly when to pick, but geographical situations, gardens, plants, and the weather can be so variable that it is impossible to give foolproof instructions.

If in doubt, pick a couple of flowers at different stages, stick on a couple of labels with, for example, 'open' and 'half-open' written on them, and dry the flowers to see what happens. One or the other will look preferable, but I confess that I rarely have the ruthlessness to throw anything out . . . it just finds its way to the back of the bunch.

There are a few very general rules that apply to most material.

Lunaria annua *(honesty)*

Removing leaves before drying

Stripping off leaves

Most flowers or greenery need to have their leaves stripped off, at least at the bottom of the stem. I tend to leave one or two leaves up by the flower head, and at least 5–7.5cm (2–3in) of leafy stem. After all, one can always strip them off later.

You must, however, always strip off leaves from the base of the stem, where the tying is done. If the material is to be propped upright, you must strip off the leaves below the upper level of the vase, leaving only bare stems within the container. Crushed leaves always look unattractive and prolong the drying time; they also cause the base of the stems to rot.

For pressing, it is wise to leave a clear 2.5cm (1in) or so of stem, otherwise there is nothing to leave as a stake for sticking into foam or attaching to wire.

ARRANGING FOR DRYING

Flowers that are to be hung, or propped upright, should be arranged on a table, or in your hands, so that the heads are not all crushed together, but staggered, and then tied up so that they look like a bunch. This will save much time later on.

Trim off the stems so that they are all the same length, as this makes storage and arranging a lot easier.

For large flowers, such as paeonia or hydrangea, hang no more than three or four together. For small flowers, such as lonas, xeranthemum, or *Centaurea cyanus*, you can arrange them into small posies, by type, so that the effect is akin to the head of a larger flower. In this way you can make almost 'instant' arrangements later on. (See the

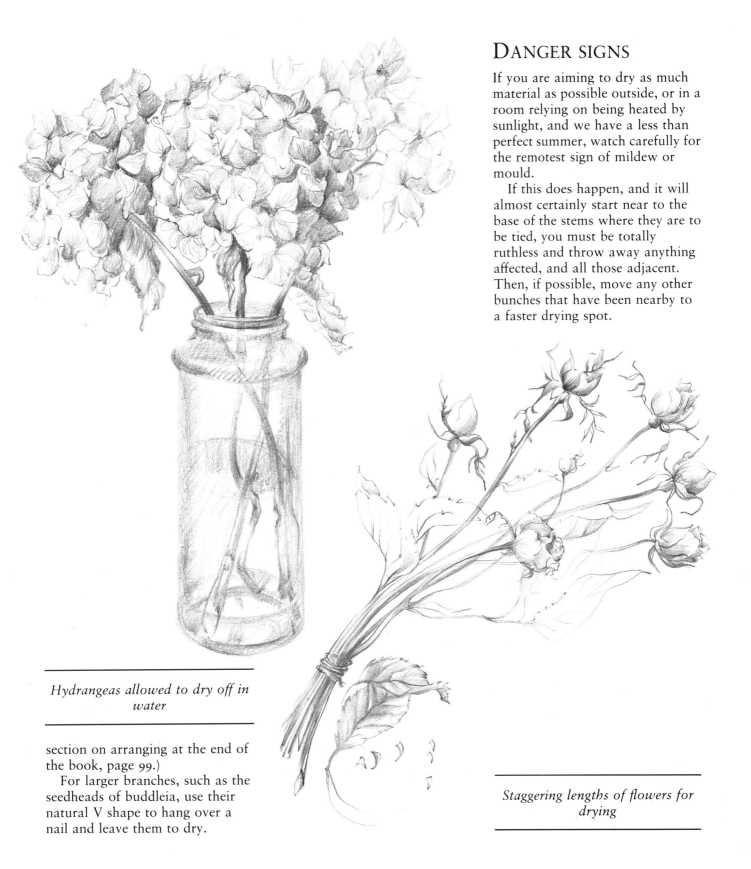

DANGER SIGNS

If you are aiming to dry as much material as possible outside, or in a room relying on being heated by sunlight, and we have a less than perfect summer, watch carefully for the remotest sign of mildew or mould.

If this does happen, and it will almost certainly start near to the base of the stems where they are to be tied, you must be totally ruthless and throw away anything affected, and all those adjacent. Then, if possible, move any other bunches that have been nearby to a faster drying spot.

Hydrangeas allowed to dry off in water

section on arranging at the end of the book, page 99.)

For larger branches, such as the seedheads of buddleia, use their natural V shape to hang over a nail and leave them to dry.

Staggering lengths of flowers for drying

Drying on a pulley

Drying on a screen

STORING AND SAVING TIME

If you have a room with a ceiling large enough to hold all your dried flowers, the easiest thing is to leave them there until they need to be used. Hung up, they can come to no damage, and will not be forgotten.

If space is limited, and you have to operate a shift system in the airing cupboard, for example, then store the dried bunches, wrapped in paper, in cardboard boxes.

As each bunch dries, wrap the flowers up, with the heads visible, so that you can remember what they are. Use wallpaper rather than newspaper; one roll of unflocked, non-vinyl, non-woodchip, pale wallpaper, or wallpaper lining paper, goes a very long way.

Try to wrap up and place the same type of flower in each box. This will mean that not only can

Circular basket filled with blue perennial delphinium, scarlet helichrysum, Stachys lanata *'Cotton boll' (lamb's tongue),* Eryngium alpinum, *solidago (golden rod) and blue hydrangea.*

you see at a glance what you have still available, but also that they are ready should you want to give a bunch or two away.

If you want to sell or give away flowers for fund-raising, very small bunches of one type of flower often fetch more than ready-mixed ones, the theory apparently being that people will buy only one mixed bunch, but several different bunches.

If you notice that there are going to be generous quantities of one type of flower, swamping everything else, it is a good idea to hang up this type in smaller bunches, despite the temptation to do the opposite. Then, when it comes to arranging, one smaller bunch of a scarcer type can be surrounded by bunches of the prolific type. Also, pre-sorted and wrapped bunches of a prolific type are excellent and easily-parted with donations for fund-raising sales.

WHERE TO DRY

Your two main concerns when considering where to dry your material are temperature and position.

Temperature

The place should remain at a constantly warm temperature of 13° to 24°C (55° to 75°F). Make sure that there is adequate ventilation, and that the atmosphere is dry. Humidity is one of your worst enemies.

Position

Darkness is ideal for drying, as the colours will stay vivid. Direct sunlight rapidly fades drying flowers. If the place cannot be totally dark, try to ensure that the material is dried out of direct sunlight.

Make sure too that the flowers are as far as possible from electric lights; these could either touch the flowers (which could cause fire) or shine directly on them for hours every day.

Try to minimize disturbance from both draughts, which might bring in damp air, and people, who might bang into them, or knock their heads on overhead bunches.

Finally, beware of toddlers, cats and playful dogs, not to mention any other curious pets. All small children and pets seem to adore the crunching sound of breaking dried material!

N.B. Please note that some seedheads are poisonous, and also that some flowers and seedheads could cause illness in anyone consuming them.

DRYING FLOWERS UPRIGHT

Outdoor shed

If you have a warm dry shed, and we enjoy a warm dry summer, (average temperature over 20°C, or 70°F), there are virtually no problems with this form of drying.

Clear as much junk out of the shed as possible, because the more dust-laden objects there are around, the more dust will settle

Drying in a shed

22

A harmony of mauves reflects the décor of this classic study and also makes an attractive all-round arrangement for a circular table. Lepidium, blue statice, blue delphinium, Stachys lanata (lamb's tongue), hydrangea, Avena sativa (oats), Papaver somniferum (poppy), and purple honesty.

on your flowers. Cover up all other objects with a dust sheet.

Make shelves for containers in which to prop material upright. They should be about 50–70cm (20–30in) deep, with about 90cm (36in) between levels. Make sure that there is space behind the shelves for air to ventilate, and that the material will not touch the outside walls. This should allow you to accommodate most types of material that need to be propped up.

It is a good idea, however, to make sure that you have some area, preferably on the ground, which can be used for very tall branches, such as angelica, seedheads of wild cow parsnip etc.

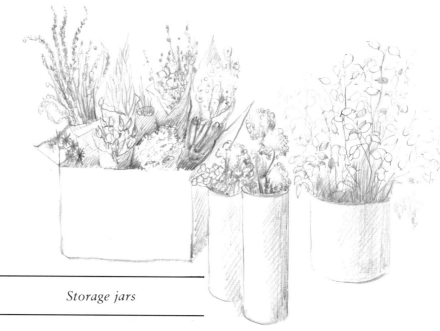

Storage jars

Airing cupboard, loft or spare bedroom

If you have no suitable shed, or it is too damp for successful drying outside, use the floor of an airing cupboard, or, if you can easily climb up and down with your booty, try the loft.

A third alternative is to use a space in a spare bedroom, either in the wardrobe, with the door slightly ajar, or in the darkest corner. You could make the corner darker by using a screen, or by constructing a makeshift one with a clotheshorse, or even a couple of chairs, covered with the darkest sheet you can find.

Containers

Plastics

Provided that the lower leaves are stripped off, plastic containers are ideal for material that is not too damp when picked. To add ventilation to the bottom of a plastic container, you could:

– punch holes in the bottom of it by tapping a sharp chisel with a hammer;
– fill it no more than a quarter full with dry pebbles, broken clay plant pots, etc.; or
– put the plastic container up on a couple of planks or bricks to ensure ventilation.

Few items you need to dry will need a larger container than a plastic bucket. Other containers could be large confectionary jars obtained from a kind-hearted shopkeeper, or large fruit juice or milk containers with their tops sawn off.

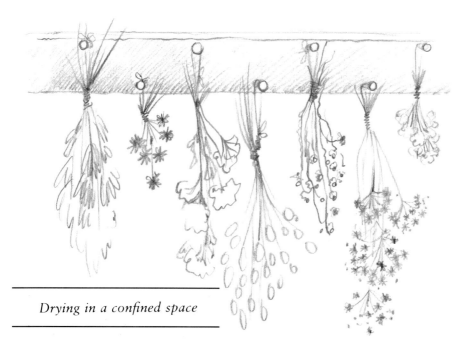

Drying in a confined space

An oval basket containing deep pink 'Dorothy Perkins' rambler roses, silvery-beige Carlina acaulis, green bamboo, green hydrangea, unpeeled purple-splotched honesty and gypsophila.

Cardboard

Cardboard boxes should be hoarded for use. Narrow, deep ones, such as cases for wine, etc. are very useful.

Ask at a carpet showroom for any surplus cardboard rolls round which carpets are rolled. Sawn into manageable lengths, they can be jammed into buckets, weighted with dry sand or stones, and used for very tall branches.

Brass, copper, baskets, etc.

If you have to dry the material in a room which is in use most of the time, and therefore you have to see the containers, then you might as well make a feature of them.

Starting with the most sumptuous, silver, brass, and even copper containers look lovely filled with drying twigs, etc. Old coal scuttles, brass kettles and chipped china wash jugs are all attractive vessels when filled. Baskets that are deep enough are also ideal, even if they are a little damaged.

Always check the base of the stems for rot, as you will probably be unwilling to punch a couple of holes in an antique brass container.

Failing all of these, or when everything decent has been filled up, you can always resort to cardboard boxes disguised with wrapping paper or wallpaper.

I once dried individually tied bunches of two or three varieties of that year's more prolific flowers, and stored them this way, and then handed over the entire box for the school sale.

DRYING FLOWERS BY HANGING

In a shed

With a warm shed, and a summer to match, your problems are minimal. Don't be tempted to hang bunches from nails in the outside walls because the walls are often very damp, owing to rising damp and falling night temperatures.

Instead, hang a pole made from the fattest piece of dowelling you can buy from your local hardware shop, a broom handle, or a plump bamboo cane. Ideally, the pole should be around eye-level or above, and suspended very firmly from the roof by wire, or that most useful of commodities, bindertwine. This should ensure that the bunches hanging down will be out of reach of the cat and inquisitive children.

Make sure that you then suspend the bunches with at least a few inches between them so that they do not touch each other.

In an airing cupboard

For people short of a shed and a decent summer, the most popular place to hang-dry is in the airing cupboard, with its hot-water tank. A room containing the central-heating boiler is also useful.

The disadvantage of most airing cupboards is their lack of space, but by hanging bunches at different levels on 7.5cm (3in) panel pins (obtainable from any hardware store) and meticulously removing fully-dried material, you will find that it can work well.

Reserve the warmest spot in your airing cupboard for drying roses, delphiniums, etc., which need to be dried as fast as possible. The warmest spot is usually closest to where the hot-water pipes lead from the tank.

In a wardrobe

With no shed and no space in the airing cupboard, there is always a possible spot in a wardrobe. Choose the sunniest, warmest room in the house and try to find a dark spot inside it. Suspend the bunches on coat hangers and leave the door slightly ajar.

In a kitchen

Many photos in the glossy magazines show attractive bunches of flowers hanging in a polished 'rustic' kitchen, often above a smooth electric hob on which nothing is ever cooking. I've never tried hanging things in the kitchen, as inevitably they would smell of sinful frying or singed toast, and the steam rising might leave them like a limp handshake; but if you have an extractor fan like the jets on Concorde, this method might work. A compromise might be to hang them as far away as possible from both cooker and sink, and in the least sunny corner.

However, things change with cookers such as an Aga or Esse, which are heated by solid fuel, oil, gas or electricity. It is the constant heat that makes all the difference.

Hang your flowers on a suspended clothes pulley, or make one from dowelling, etc., as shown on page 20. Alternatively, knock panel pins into exposed beams at least 30cm (1ft) apart.

WARNING *When material is fully dry, it has the properties of tinder, so make absolutely sure that you leave nothing within a metre of a gas cooker, gas fire, open fire, or electric bar fire.*

Drying in an oven

Oven drying (for electric ovens only)

A few plants need to be dried so fast that only the oven will do. Some other material, such as cones, fungi, and moss, can be conveniently dried this way, but it is not essential.

The annual cornflower, *Centaurea cyanus*, is an example of a flower that will dry well almost only in an oven. If you have an electric oven, remove all but the top wire shelf and tie the bunch onto this. Set the oven at the lowest temperature. If the oven has a fan, close the door and wait for at least half an hour before the material is totally dry; if the oven has no fan, try leaving the door ajar and checking every ten minutes or so.

With a constant-heat oven (Aga, Esse, etc.), lay the flowers on a baking tray, with the heads propped up on the tray edge, and leave in the coolest part of the oven, either for several hours or overnight. Only trial and error will reveal the correct length of time, as it depends very much on the moisture content of the plant when picked.

Tying material for hanging
The most convenient and easiest ties to use are elastic bands, balls of wool (real wool is easier to break than synthetics), and wire, such as florists' wire, or even wire used for tying plastic bags can go round thin stems.

If you use wire or elastic bands, you have to hang the bunch as if it were a clothespeg. If you use wool ties, you can leave a long loop, and hang things at different heights, which allows you to fit much more in a confined space. Allow at least a space the size of the average bunch between material.

Be sure to tie firmly and tightly, especially with wool, as the stems will shrink remarkably during the drying process, and you do not want to find your flowers falling down on the floor.

Place a sheet of newspaper or an old sheet underneath drying seedheads to catch the seeds when the pods open.

PRESSING

If you have started reading this book from the beginning, you will probably have gathered that I advise drying as many leaves which will retain their colour as possible.

Pressing is the most successful way for the vast majority of leaves, though most experts on drying flowers tend to discount pressing, as they maintain that leaves are left too flat and rigid. I have found, however, that, while many do remain as flat as boards for a short time, most will bend and curl slightly when *in situ*, or stay looking attractively floppy: this lends a pleasingly relaxed air to most arrangements.

In books, under magazines, etc.
This is suitable for small leaves only. Pick all leaves to be pressed on a good dry day, leaving on a small amount of stalk so that there is something to stick into the foam eventually. Place in between sheets of blotting paper and allow plenty of book pages between leaves. Pile other books or heavy weights on top and leave for at least a couple of weeks in a temperature above 13°C (55°F).

Under carpets
If you have a loose, unfitted carpet, as opposed to a fireside rug, and one that is not on the main runway through the house, use this for pressing.

Roll back the carpet, lay several layers of newspaper on the floor, put down the material to be pressed, cover with at least another half-dozen layers of paper, and re-cover with carpet. Don't skimp on the amount of newspaper on top: not only do you need plenty to absorb the moisture from the leaves, but too few layers can mean that the woven imprint of the carpet will decorate your leaves. It is simply the convenience of the carpet, not the weight, that makes it a useful medium for pressing.

Pressing layers of leaves between newspaper under the carpet

Under furniture

You can use space under sofas, large armchairs or beds, or any item of furniture under which you can push material but that is unlikely to be moved.

To make it easier to insert and pull out wadges of pressed material from under furniture, I made a 'rug' of thick layers of paper stapled together, and firmed up on either side with bamboo sticks. The effect was rather like a stretcher. This made a container large enough almost to fill up the space under the bed. Alternatively, you could simply use trays or slender

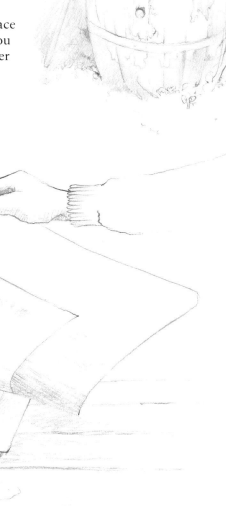

Lavender basket filled with deep blue-purple Limonium sinuatum *(annual statice), blue hydrangea, seedheads of* Papaver somniferum *(poppies), cream helichrysum, green seedheads of* Avena sativa *(oats).*

planks of insulating board or hardboard cut to fit under sofas or armchairs.

On any of these items place at least a couple of layers of newspaper, lay out the leaves, cover with at least half a dozen layers of paper, and leave for at least a week or so.

The drying time depends on the temperature, plus the amount of moisture inherent in the material.

Preparing material

Generally speaking, the earlier you start pressing leaves, the better: the fresher and younger the material, the longer is its staying power. However, it is often too taxing to rush out and save early spring leaves when it just appears that

A large arrangement prepared for a dark hall. The reds and yellows not only pick out the flowers in the picture hanging over the stairs, but match the vibrancy of décor and eastern influence throughout the house. Bamboo, delphinium, Eryngium × oliverianum, Eryngium alpinum, Achillea filipendulina, *red dyed achillea, red roses, leek seed heads, solidaster,* Carthamus tinctorius, Carlina acaulis, *hydrangea.*

winter has vanished, and the next one is mercifully a long way off.

Many leaves press well in the mid- to late summer, and you should save plenty of space for the early autumn colours, which can preserve perfectly. *Fagus sylvatica* 'Cuprea' (copper beech), paeonia (paeony) leaves, and clumps of the red-tinged polygonum leaves press beautifully.

Ruthlessly reject any material that has blemishes, since these magnify when dried.

Prepare the material by smoothing out the leaves and pinching off overlapping leaves, so that everything to be dried is only one leaf-layer thick. Be fairly disciplined about pinching or cutting off overlapping leaves. In the end, sparsely-leaved twigs look a lot better than layers of squashed leaves. Strip off lower leaves on, for example, the ferns, so that you make sure there is enough stalk left either to stick directly into foam, or to attach to a wire.

Lay everything out so that it does not touch. Cover up with layers of paper, carpet, etc. Do not worry about putting weight on top so much as adding layers of absorbent paper: it is this that dries them.

You may find that as the summer wears on, and the 'phone rings for the umpteenth time while you are laying the final row of leaves, some material will have been dried with creases in it. Don't, as one new enthusiast tried to do, bother to try ironing them. The odd few creases can look charming . . .

PLANTS

NOTES ON TERMS USED IN THE PLANT DESCRIPTIONS

'Any seed merchant' means the vendor of packets of seeds – local nurseries, local shops which sell hardware and gardening equipment, etc., and even the local shops that sells seeds only in the spring time.

'More specialist seed merchant' usually means a vendor who sells seeds by post. Some suggested addresses are given on pages 123 and 124.

ANNUALS

ALTHAEA ROSEA
(hollyhock)

Confusingly, hollyhocks can be grown as biennials, or as perennials, but most of the seeds now on offer are described as annuals. Generally, the latter offer the best results for flowers for drying.

Both flowers and seedheads can be used for drying. Deep pink or red double flowers work best for drying, as pale colours fade too much. Seeds available from any seed merchant.

I once saw a huge empty fireplace in a Scottish castle filled with nothing but hollyhocks, set into the fire basket. A grand plant for a grand setting, but worth trying in less magnificent settings!

Cultivation
Sow seeds in summer for transplanting to next year's flowering sites in autumn. Plant in a sunny sheltered site with, if possible, a wall or tall hedge to lend support; plants might otherwise need staking. Height up to 1.8m (6ft); planting distance 37.5–45cm (15–18in).

Preparation
Cut when the flowers at the base of the stem are fully out, and others nearly out, but the top flowers still tightly closed; this should ensure maximum flower retention. The bottom flowers may fall or need to be cut off for hanging. Hang upside down.

Alternatively, wait until the seed-pods have formed and cut then, hanging them upside down. The individual florets can be cut off and dried on wires or placed right way up on a piece of chicken wire or wire cake-tray.

ALYSSUM MARITIMUM

Low-growing annual, easily grown from seed, obtainable from most nurseries as bedding plants. Both flowers and seedheads can be used for drying.

Cultivation
Sow seeds under glass in March; transplant in early summer. Put in sunny spot, ordinary soil, or in hanging baskets or pots. Grows to a height of 10–15cm (3–6in); planting distance 20–30cm (8–12in).

Preparation
Cut when the flowers are nearly out, and hang upside down, or wait until the seedheads appear; this is either at the end of the summer, or after a period of drought.

AMARANTHUS CAUDATUS
(love-lies-bleeding)

Drooping flower stems come in deep pink, maroon, and green versions. The version 'Green Thumb', which is a vivid green, does well. Grow from seed, obtainable from most seed merchants. Less likely to be obtained as a bedding plant. The flower stems are used for drying. These slightly drooping, languid flowers are perfect for unusual arrangements, overhanging baskets, etc., and are one of the few flowers that remain flexible when dry.

Cultivation
Sow seeds under glass in spring, transplant in early summer to a warm, sheltered spot. Seldom need staking, but will suffer from mud splashes in very rainy weather. Height 60cm (2ft); planting distance 30cm (1ft).

Preparation
Cut from base of stem when the flowers are just out. Remove some leaves at foot, and hang upside down. Important to cut the green versions before they are fully out, otherwise they will turn fluffy and pale.

AMMOBIUM ALATUM
(winged everlasting)

Snaking flower stems are topped with tiny pure-white daisy-like flowers. Only possible to grow from seeds, obtainable from more specialist seed merchants. This is one of the few flowers to remain truly white. Picking when the yellow centres are fully out, or after a lot of rain, can result in dark brown centres.

Cultivation
Sow seeds under glass in late spring. This is usually a prolific cropper, and a dozen plants are more than enough for most gardens. Plant in full sun, or partial shade. Height up to 60cm (2ft); planting distance 30cm (1ft).

Preparation
Cut when the top flower is just opening and revealing the yellow-spotted centre. Leave a stem of 20cm (8in) or so. Later in the year, pick off as soon as they

1 Althaea rosea
2 Alyssum maritimum
3 Amaranthus candatus
4 Ammobium alatum

1 *Briza*
2 Calendula officinalis
3 Carthamus tinctorius
4 Celosia argentea plumosa

flower, as supply usually exceeds picking enthusiasm. Slightly awkward stems respond well to the 'gathering in the bunch' principle. Place the heads together, tie on a rubber band or wool just underneath, and tie again at the base of the stems. Hang upside down.

ATRIPLEX HORTENSIS

These tall spikes of deep red or vivid green flowers are rather like sophisticated versions of dock in flower. Obtainable from more specialist seed merchants. The flower spikes are used for drying. The green retains its vivid colouring, making it an invaluable part of many arrangements.

Cultivation
Sow in boxes in late spring, or directly into the soil where you want it to flower, in full sun, or partial shade. Height up to 1.5m (5ft); planting distance 37.5cm (15in).

Preparation
Cut when the spikes are fully mature and hang upside down.

BRIZA MAXIMA
(large quaking grass, or pearl grass)

Rustling grass with small pear-shaped heads. Grow from seed obtainable from many seed merchants, or sometimes in packets containing several different varieties. This is one of the very special grasses, useful for lightening and softening arrangements, and which will continue to rustle and move with light breezes and draughts in the house.

Cultivation
Sow seeds in sunny site where they are to flower in late spring. Not really necessary to thin out. Ordinary soil. Height up to 50cm (20in).

Preparation
Cut when the seedheads are well formed; pick from base of stem. Hang upside down.

CALENDULA OFFICINALIS
(pot marigold)

Bright orange heads of simple pot marigolds dry well for colour, but bear little resemblance to the original, as they shrivel and close up somewhat. Seeds available from any seed merchant. They increase voraciously, so a few plants will give bounteous rewards. They are so easy to grow that, even if they are not outstanding dried, they are worth gathering for bulking out an arrangement.

Cultivation
Sow the seeds in poor or ordinary soil, in a sunny position. (Poor soil encourages more flowers per plant.) Choose the spot carefully, for they will self-seed and spread. Height up to 60cm (2ft); thin out to 20cm (8in).

Preparation
Cut when the flower heads have just opened wide. Cut from the base of the stem, leaving on leaves around the flower head, which appears to help keep the flower from dropping. Hang upside down. The bright heads can be placed upside down on a wire tray, minus stem, for popping into small arrangements, gluing, or pot pourri.

CARTHAMUS TINCTORIUS

Intriguing plant, not often grown, which used to be used for dyeing. The fat green heads, very attractive as they are for drying, also sprout orange thistle-like tufts. Obtainable from more specialist seed merchants. Grow these for their novelty value and also for their useful green colour. The orange is almost a bonus!

Cultivation
Sow the seeds in spring under glass, as they do need a long growing season. Plant out in early summer in ordinary soil, the most sheltered and sunniest position possible. Not a certainty for heavy cropping. Height up to 90cm (3ft); plant 30cm (1ft) apart.

Preparation
Cut when the flowers are producing the orange fluffy petals. If they do not flower by the end of the season, pick them as they are, or transplant into a greenhouse!

CELOSIA ARGENTEA PLUMOSA

(Sometimes listed under Amaranthus.) Flower plumes of this rather tender annual produce startling colours of bright oranges, scarlets, and yellows. Not usually available as a bedding plant. Grow from seed, available from more specialist seed merchants; can also be grown in pots. Often used in bedding schemes in public parks; ask for flower stems when they are being thrown away at the end of the summer.

Cultivation
Sow seeds in February or March under glass. Harden off carefully in a cold frame; plant out in a

sheltered and very sunny position in early summer. Can suffer in a cold, wet summer. Height up to 60cm (2ft); space 30cm (1ft) apart. If grown in pots, will need feeding regularly.

Preparation

Cut from the base of the stem when the main central flower spike is fully out. Hang upside down, either singly or in groups of no more than three, as they are substantial flowers to dry.

CENTAUREA CYANUS (cornflower)

Utterly reliable annual, famous for the deep blue of its flowers, but also available in violet, mauve, pink, and white. Seed available from most seed merchants. Cornflowers are one of the best flowers for retaining their blue, which, when dried, they do for a couple of years. They go well with all pinks and the yellows of lonas and achillea.

Cultivation

Sow seeds under glass in late spring, or direct into the flowering site in early summer. Grow in any soil, in a fairly sunny position. Height up to 60cm (2ft); plant 20cm (8in) apart.

Preparation

Cut each of the flowers as they open out fully; this is a rather time-consuming job, but careful picking will ensure a good crop and encourage flowering until cut down by frost.

Cornflowers need to be dried in an oven (see p. 27), as this is the only definite way to ensure that they retain their colour. Dried more slowly, some of their petals turn grey and eventually drop off;

flowers not quite out will often not open.

CRASPEDIA UNIFLORA

Pompons of yellow/orange flowers top bare stems. Seed obtainable from more specialist seed merchants. Their quite delightful shape and colour make them worth growing, even if the results can sometimes look rather sparse.

Cultivation

Sow the seed under glass in late spring for planting out in summer. Grow in ordinary garden soil, in a sunny site. Small and pretty enough to pop in among a border of mixed flowers. Height up to 45cm (18in); planting distance about 20cm (8in).

Preparation

Cut when the flower heads are nearly out, and hang upside down. If you are a little late, and the heads start to look rather downy, then spray with hair lacquer.

DELPHINIUM CONSOLIDA (larkspur)

Come in several shades of blues, indigo violets, pinks, and white. Seed available from most seed merchants.

This is one of the best-value plants to grow for drying, although bad summers can wreak havoc. A large arrangement composed solely of annual and perennial delphiniums is stunning, very easy, and effective. The twisting, elegant shapes of larkspur also lend themselves well to hanging bunches.

Cultivation

Sow seeds in autumn for planting

out the following spring, or under glass in spring for planting out in the summer. Has the reputation of not transplanting well, but this can be solved by sowing seeds in small pots, thus lessening root disturbance. Plant in good garden soil, enriched with compost, in a sunny site and well sheltered.

Larkspur can be blown over by strong winds and lots of rain, and therefore muddied, so it is best to stake it. Height up to 45cm (18in); planting distance 30cm (1ft).

Preparation

Cut when the top half of flower stem is still tightly closed. Strip off the lower leaves, and hang the stems upside down in the warmest part of the airing cupboard.

GOMPHRENA GLOBOSA (globe amaranth)

Small, cone-shaped flowers akin to clover come in bright magenta pinks, and white. Seed available from more specialist seed merchants.

The small flower heads are ideal for posies.

Cultivation

Sow under glass in spring for planting out in summer, either in a sunny spot in ordinary soil, or in pots. Height up to 30cm (1ft); planting distance 15cm (6in).

Preparation

Cut when the flowers are fully out on short stems, and hang them upside down.

GYPSOPHILA ELEGANS

Beloved of flower arrangers when classically mixed with roses and sweet peas. Lovely for combining

1 Centaurea cyanus
2 Craspedia uniflora
3 Delphinium consolida
4 Gomphrena globosa
5 Gypsophila elegans

1 Helichrysum '*Monstrosum*'
2 Helichrysum '*Subulifolium*'
3 Helipterum humboldtianum
4 Helipterum manglesii
5 *Iberis*

42

with almost any other dried flower, and equally pretty alone. Seed available from most seed merchants. Choose double-flowered varieties.

Cultivation

Sow in pots under glass in late spring for planting out in the summer, or directly into the flowering site. Possible to make several sowings throughout the summer for continuous picking. Any soil and reasonably sunny position. Height up to 45cm (18in); planting distance 30cm (1ft).

Preparation

Cut off at the base of the stem when some of the flowers are fully out, and hang upside down.

HELICHRYSUM
(everlasting, or straw flower)

Of daisy-like appearance, and the mainstay of the dried flower garden, there are a confusing number of these plants now listed, often under different names in different catalogues.

The annual species, *H. bracteatum*, produces large white flowers that are tinged with pink and cream. Cultivars within this species are 'Monstrosum' (large double flowers), 'Monstrosum Double Height', 'Nanum' (a dwarf form), and 'Dwarf Spangle Mixed'. Colours are deep red, pinks, terracotta, orange, white and pale yellow.

Most are obtainable in a packet of mixed colours from any seed merchant, very occasionally available as bedding plants, and packets of one colour only are available from more specialist seed merchants. If you want to grow enough flowers for drying to supply Christmas presents, fêtes, etc., then buy the seeds by colour in separate packets; by hanging separate colours together, it simplifies arranging considerably.

'Subulifolium' is a separate strain descended from *H. bracteatum* and produces only bright yellow, shiny, daisy-like flowers.

It is best to keep track of new seeds on offer from more specialist seed merchants.

Cultivation

Sow seeds under glass in late spring for planting out in early summer, in a sunny, fairly sheltered site, in good garden soil. Dwarf varieties make good plants for tubs. Height range from 90cm (3ft) for *H. bracteatum*; 45–120cm (18in–4ft) for *H.b.* 'Monstrosum'; 30cm (1ft) for the dwarf varieties, and 38cm (15in) for *H.b.* 'Subulifolium'. Plant around 30–38cm (12–15in) apart.

Preparation

Most instructions maintain that cutting the flowers is best done when the outer two rows of petals are out, and the interior part of the flower still tightly closed. This is certainly ideal, but if the flower heads have opened a little further, pick them anyway. Some open ones look lovely. If, after drying, these very opened ones look untidy or faded, as they occasionally do, add them to pot pourri for colour.

Pick with a stem no more than 15cm (6in) long, bunch together and hang upside down. Or, pick off the heads only, and wire immediately, stabbing the end of the wire into foam, so that the flowers are upright.

Stalkless heads can also be dried at a low temperature in a solid fuel or electric oven (*not* a gas one), or in a microwave, placed on paper towels, for no more than two minutes at maximum power. They can then be used for pot pourri or gluing.

If the heads fall off when drying, it is usually because they are too wet. If the heads are still usable, then wire them; if not, discard them. Heads that were too wet when picked, even though this may not have been obvious at the time, tend to rot from the centre. If this happens, discard them immediately.

HELIPTERUM

Another mainstay of flower drying, with names that are often confused. *H. humboldtianum* has balls of tiny yellow flowers; *H. manglesii* (once known as *Rhodanthe manglesii*) has small nodding heads of pink or white daisy-like heads, on thread-thin stems, silvery on the outside of the petals, and *H. roseum* (once *Acroclinium roseum*) has large, daisy-style flowers that have more vivid colouring in pinks and white, with a yellow centre, which sometimes has a dark brown spot. The stems have tiny, distinctive thread-like leaves.

All are easy and rewarding to grow for cutting, the flowers from *H. roseum* retaining their bright, fresh colours for years, the pink being one of the best of all dried flowers.

Cultivation

Sow under glass in late spring, planting out in early summer in a sunny spot, ordinary soil. *H. manglesii* does not often transplant well, and should be sown in small pots to lessen root disturbance. If they are slow to show much progress when planted outside, then cover with a cloche.

Preparation
H. humboldtianum should be picked with short stems, no more than 5–7.5cm (2–3in), when the tiny centres of the florets within the pompon flower are just opening out. Hang upside down.

Cut *H. manglesii* when they are fully out, and hang upside down. If this is rather fiddly, you can cut from the base of the stem, including half-opened buds. These will seldom open, but the undersides will still look attractively silvery. The colours on *H. manglesii* will fade within a few months.

H. roseum should be picked from the base of the stem when fully out, leaves stripped off, if possible, and hung upside down. They retain their colour very well.

IBERIS
(candytuft)

Pink, white, and pale purple flowers in flattish heads give way to spectacular seedheads, which can be dried when green. Grow from seeds obtainable from any seed merchant; they will self-seed happily.

Seedheads retain their green colour for a long time, eventually fading to cream. Can be used as props for flower heads of other species, or sprayed gold or silver for Christmas.

Cultivation
Sow the seeds in spring in their flowering site, preferably in a sunny or lightly-shaded spot where their ability to self-seed can be put to advantage. Will grow on poor soil, in among small gravel, and in tubs. Height up to 20cm (8in); thin out to same distance apart.

Preparation
Cut when the green seedheads are just formed. The larger plants produce seedheads which are quite delightful and should be stuck upright into foam.

LIMONIUM
(statice)

There are three quite dissimilar species of annual statice: *L. bonduellii* produces yellow flowers; *L. sinuatum*, which is the best known, has arched sprays of purple flowers, and is also available in pinks, magenta, apricot, and yellow, and *L. suworowii* throws up thin stems of pink-covered flowers that twist into intriguing shapes. The colours of both *L. sinuatum* and *L. suworowii* remain vivid for years. *L. bonduellii* is available from more specialist seed merchants, *L. sinuatum* and *L. suworowii* from most seed merchants.

Cultivation
All should be sown under glass in spring, to be planted out in early summer. Sometimes the results from seeds can be very disappointing. Plant out in a very sunny site, in ordinary soil. *L. sinuatum* needs a long season in which to flower, so early planting (as soon as all danger of frost is past) is advisable. Height 30–45cm (12–18in); planting distance around 15–20cm (6–8in).

Preparation
Cut when the flowers of *L. bonduellii* and *L. sinuatum* are fully out, as they rarely open well after picking. Hang upside down, or prop up *L. sinuatum* in a vase, leaving room for air to circulate round the base of the stems, and prevent mould forming. It is unnecessary to try to strip off the 'wings' on the leaves.

L. suworowii usually crops well, and the flowers can be picked when either partially or fully out. The spires can grow to 30cm (1ft) and it may be more useful to pick when they are less lengthy. Hang upside down, or stick the stalks into a block of foam for drying.

LINUM USITATISSIMUM
(flax)

The common flax produces brilliant blue flowers that turn into fat, twinkling seedheads, which are some of the best to dry. Wonderful for lightening arrangements instead of gypsophila, and can be sprayed to good effect. Very easily grown. Seed obtainable from most seed merchants.

Cultivation
Sow in the flowering site, in ordinary soil, full sun, and thin out to 38cm (15in) apart. Height maximum of 90cm (3ft).

Preparation
Cut down the entire plant, or large branch, when the seedheads are fully formed, and hang upside down.

1 Limonium sinuatum
2 Limonium suworowii
3 Linum usitatissimum

1 Lonas inodora
2 Lunaria annua
3 Nicandra physalodes
4 Moluccella laevis

LONAS INODORA
(African daisy)

Not a well-known plant, *Lonas inodora* has plump primrose-yellow flowers which go well with cornflowers, and other small flowers. Very easy to grow from seed, obtainable from more specialist seed merchants, and ideal as an edging plant for a border. Survives well in even the coolest summer. Quite time-consuming to pick.

Cultivation
Sow the seeds under glass in spring for planting out in early summer, in ordinary soil, in a sunny position. Height up to 45cm (18in); planting distance 20cm (8in).

Preparation
Cut when the small clusters of flowers at the tips of each branching stem are fully out. This is one of the few flowers that do not suffer from being left too long before picking; but beware a wet summer, for they can turn mustard yellow after too much rain. Hang upside down. As the flowers are so tiny, they benefit well from bunching and are therefore suitable for posies.

LUNARIA ANNUA
(honesty)

Really a biennial, but included here as an annual as it can usually be persuaded to flower in the same year. Has a resolute tendency to spread rapidly through self-seeding, and should be sown only in an out-of-the-way place in a large garden.

The purple/pink flowers give way to round seedpods, which can be picked when green, tinged with purple. Only the purple-flowered variety produces purple-blotched pods. If left until the pods turn brown/white, the outer skins can be rubbed off with the fingers, and the silvery-white shells are left, reminiscent of glass-domed Victorian displays.

A beautiful variegated version, with green/cream-blotched leaves and seedpods is also available; the seeds can be obtained from more specialist seed merchants.

Unless you have the space, see if you can find a garden with a good crop of honesty and ask to pick there. I always collect as much as I decently can from friends and dry it green, as soon as the pods have formed. A large bunch will make a very easy 'tree' if you attach foam to the top of a pole and spike it with branches of all roughly the same length.

Cultivation
Sow the seeds in summer for flowering the following year in poor, or ordinary, garden soil, in any position except very deep shade. Height about 75cm (30in); planting distance the same.

Preparation
Cut when the seedpods have just formed and are still green, with the odd flower still showing at the top, or wait until they have gone white. At both times, cut from the base of the stem, peel off any leaves, and prop upright, or hang upside down.

If some flowers are still out, they will shrivel as they dry, leaving this attractive speck of colour. If you want white pods, rub off the outer layer of brown skin, and this and the seeds will fall away quite readily. Retain the seeds for planting out.

MOLUCCELLA LAEVIS
(bells of Ireland)

Flower stems produce 'bells' which contain the true, insignificant white flower. Sow from seed, generally obtainable from any seed merchant.

The marvellous clear green of the bells lasts for only a few months, and then only if out of all direct sunlight. Then the colour changes to an almost opalescent soft cream that preserves for years. They are very brittle at this stage, so it is best to arrange early and leave well alone!

Cultivation
Sow the seeds under glass in spring, for planting out as soon as danger of frost is past. Plant out in well-drained, sunny position, in ordinary garden soil. Protect from slugs if necessary. They often need a long growing season, and suffer in wet, cold summers, never reaching their full size. Height up to 45cm (18in); planting distance 30cm (1ft).

Preparation
Cut when the small white flower in the centre of the 'bell' is out, and peel off leaves and some of the unformed bells at the top. Hang upside down.

NICANDRA PHYSALODES
(shoo-fly plant)

Not a well-known plant, but one that is very easy to grow from seed obtainable from more specialist seed merchants. The seedpods that follow the indigo blue, white-centred flowers, are like green parcels, splitting to reveal a shiny brown ball of seeds.

The wonderful shiny pods are a happy addition to almost any arrangement, and few dried plants are truly as luminous.

Cultivation

Either sow under glass in spring, planting out at the beginning of summer, or sow directly into the flowering site. Sunny spot, ordinary garden soil, and with plenty of space to accommodate their growth, often up to 120cm (4ft); planting distance 30cm (1ft).

Preparation

Cut when several of the green seed parcels have formed, cutting off at the base of the stem. Remove leaves, any flowers and immature seedpods. Hang upside down to dry. Be sure to cut fairly regularly during the growing period, as the green pods soon turn brown when hung up if they have been formed for more than a few weeks, or during a rainy spell. Leaving the pods growing on the stems for longer leads to the pods becoming attractively skeletonized. The lower pods, which have to be removed to leave a bare stem for arranging, can be wired (see page 100).

NIGELLA DAMASCENA (love-in-a-mist)

Aptly-named plant, which has blue or other jewel-coloured flowers followed by almost square seedpods, which are green with splotches of purple. Obtainable from any seed merchant.

Whole arrangements can be made from love-in-a-mist. The ease with which they grow makes them first-class value – even when planted by children, who delight in their fast growing and changing stages.

Cultivation

Sow the seeds direct into the flowering site, in a sunny spot, in ordinary garden soil. Height up to 60cm (2ft); thin to 10cm (4in) apart.

Preparation

Cut from the base of the stem when some of the seedpods have formed. No need to bother about stripping the leaves, unless from the lower 10cm (4in), where they are to be tied up. Often some flowers will still be out, and frequently they will dry into a shrunken speck of the same brilliant colour. Hang upside down to dry.

PAPAVER (poppy)

Of all the varieties of poppies available, *P. somniferum* produces the large seedheads that dry best. Available from most seed merchants.

Poppy seedheads are very easy to produce, and a fat handful bunched together ally well with small spindly flowers.

Cultivation

Sow the seeds where you want them to flower, in a sunny open site, in ordinary garden soil. They can also be sown under glass in late spring for planting out in summer. Height up to 90cm (3ft); thin seedlings to 10cm (4in) apart.

Preparation

Cut when the seedheads are fully formed and greeny-blue. Cut off at the base of the stem, remove all leaves, and hang upside down. Leaving the heads on the plant for too long, especially during a rainy period, leads to them turning beige/grey. Pods picked too early

will shrivel. Some experimenting may be necessary!

SALVIA HORMINUM (clary)

Good value for fresh arrangements. When dried, the top leaf bracts, which turn violet, magenta, pink, or white, shrivel considerably, but retain their colour. The secret is to mass salvias in containers to obtain best value from the richly-coloured but rather shrivelled results. Easily grown from seed available from most seed merchants.

Cultivation

Sow the seeds either in the flowering site or under glass in late spring, for planting out in early summer. Will continue flowering until cut down by frost. Plant in ordinary garden soil, well-drained, in a sunny or lightly-shaded position. Height up to 45cm (18in); planting distance 23cm (9in).

Preparation

Cut when the bracts are well coloured. Chop off from the base of the stem, very carefully stripping off the lower leaves, as the tender stems snap easily. Hang upside down.

SCABIOSA STELLATA (scabious or pincushion flower)

Wishy-washy pale mauve flowers produce astonishing seedheads of slightly-prickly bronzes with touches of purple. Easily grown from seed obtainable from more specialist seed merchants.

Cultivation

Either sow seeds directly in the

1 Nigella damascena
2 Papaver somniferum
3 Salvia horminum
4 Scabiosa stellata
5 Xeranthemum annuum

flowering site, or plant them under glass in spring, to plant out in early summer. Good sunny spot in ordinary garden soil. Height 20cm (8in); thin to 7.5cm (3in) apart.

Preparation
Cut when the seedheads have formed, cutting off at the base of the stem for that seedhead only. Hang upside down.

Unusual drumstick heads are very useful for filling in arrangements in deep reds, copper colours, etc., when it is possible to cheat slightly and use the seedheads, removed from their stems if necessary, and stuck onto other material.

Sailing boats and reeds on the Tay

XERANTHEUM ANNUUM (everlasting flower)

Spindly-flowered plant with flowers in deep lilac, pink, and white. The daisy-like flowers bunched together are very useful for simple arrangements. Easily grown from seed obtainable from more specialist seed merchants.

Cultivation
Sow either directly into the soil where you want it to flower, or under glass in late spring for planting out in early summer. Ordinary garden soil, full sun to light shade. Height up to 60cm (2ft); planting distance 30cm (1ft).

Preparation
Cut when each flower at the end of its bare stem is in full flower. Half-open buds do not open, and flowers that have been open for a week or so, or subject to rain, often turn rather dull. Rather a fiddly flower to pick, and if at the end of the season there is still a good selection of flowers left, then try chopping off the whole plant just above soil level and then dealing with the flowers.

Corn stocks and Scabius lona

Old cart and eryngium

PERENNIALS, BIENNIALS, BULBS AND SMALL SHRUBS

ACANTHUS MOLLIS
(bear's breeches)

The leaves, which have been used for centuries as the model for carving on plaster and furniture, can be pressed. The bold flower stems, with their deep pinky-purple and white flowers dry well, and for arrangements of heroic proportions, both leaves and flowers are first class. Plants are obtainable from most nurseries.

Cultivation
Plant during dormant months in sun or light shade, where they can be left for several years, until they need subdividing. Height up to 90cm (3ft); planting distance 60cm (2ft).

Preparation
Cut the leaves at any time in the summer or early autumn, chopping off from the base of the leaf stalk and pressing. The flowers should be cut from the base of the stem when the petals are fully unfurled three-quarters of the way up the stem. Hang upside down.

ACHILLEA
(yarrow)

Two varieties of achillea can be dried. *A. filipendulina* has grey/silver aromatic foliage and produces flat yellow heads, composed of clusters of tiny flowers. Hybrids of *A. filipendulina* and similar types dry only if yellow. *A. ptarmica* is quite different, and has small round white flower heads. Choose the double-flowered version.

Both can usually be obtained as plants from most nurseries. If *A. ptarmica* is not easily available as a plant, it can be grown with success from seed, obtainable from more specialist seed merchants.

Cultivation
Both can be sown during the dormant season in an open, well-drained, sunny site in ordinary garden soil. Divide by root during the same period when the plants become too large. *A. filipendulina* grows to between 90–160cm (3–5ft); planting distance 90cm (3ft); *A. ptarmica* to 75cm (30in); planting distance 38cm (15in).

Preparation
Cut when the flat yellow flower heads of *A. filipendulina* are fully out. If in doubt, later is preferable to earlier, as only when the tiny florets are wide open will they dry well: too early, and the florets shrivel. Cut with as long stem as wished (they can always be shortened later) and hang upside down. If the florets do start to shrivel, then prop upright in a jar with a tiny amount of water to 'mature'.

A. ptarmica needs to be picked from the base of the stem; strip off lower leaves when the flowers are almost all out. This will vary from the top ones being almost over to the lower ones being not quite out. Pick anyway, and if the top ones turn brown when drying, chop them off. Hang upside down.

ACONITUM
(monkshood)

Aconitums produce spires of deep blue/violet flowers, the varieties *A. napellus* and *A. wilsonii* being worth growing for drying. Plants are usually available from most nurseries.

Avoid varieties that have bicolour flowers, which are often blue tinged with white, as these do not succeed so well. White and yellow are available, which might dry.

Tricky to grow from seed. *All types of aconitum are poisonous.*

Cultivation
Plant in damp, rich soil, in a shaded or partially shaded position during the dormant period. Height up to 1.5m (5ft); planting distance 45cm (18in).

Preparation
Cut when the flower spires are almost fully out, strip off the leaves and hang upside down in the warmest place you have. If some of the flowers have gone to seed on the flower spire, it is still possible to rescue the smaller flower shoots which branch off and to dry those individually.

The seedheads also dry well, usually retaining the green colour, but often splitting to disgorge the seeds.

1

4

2

3

53

1 Adiantum pedatum
2 Alchemilla mollis
3 *Allium seedheads and flowers*
4 Anaphalis margaritacea

ADIANTUM
(maidenhair fern)

This is one of the most special of ferns, ideal for framing arrangements containing smaller flowers, such as *Centaurea cyanus*, *Armeria maritima*, helipterums, etc. The delicate leaves of *A. pedatum* and *A. venustum*, both hardy in Britain, press very well. Plants are sometimes obtainable from local nurseries, more certainly from specialist sources.

Cultivation
In almost any location, in light shade or full sun, adiantums will find space for their roots in between the cracks of walls. Plant any time in the late summer to spring. Height up to 30cm (1ft); planting distance the same.

Preparation
Cut when the green leaves have just formed, before any sign of the feathery insignificant flower appears. Press.

ALCHEMILLA MOLLIS
(lady's mantle)

Excellent-value plant, as the exquisitely-shaped leaves can be pressed, and the lime/yellow-green misty clusters of flowers dry very well. Provides plenty to cut, and the flowers are valuable for their retention of colour, as well as for filling in and bulking out arrangements. Plants are easily obtainable from any nursery; self-seeds happily.

Cultivation
Plant during the dormant season ideally, although alchemillas are so tough that they can even be transplanted carefully when in flower. They like a damp, partially shaded site, and one in which they can spread undisturbed. Good front of border or path plant. Height 30cm (1ft); planting distance 38cm (15in).

Preparation
Cut from the base of the stem when the flowers are nearly fully formed. Hang upside down to dry. The leaves can be pressed at any time from early summer onwards.

ALLIUM
(ornamental onions)

A. aflatunense, *A. albopilosum*, *A. moly*, *A. sphaerocephalon*, and *A. giganteum* all produce drumstick flower heads that can be dried when in flower or in seed. Other ornamental onions can be used in the same way. Smaller varieties can be planted in tubs. Bulbs are obtainable from most nurseries; they are easy to grow, and well worth it for the unusual shapes.

Cultivation
Alliums need an open, well-drained site, where they can be left to increase from the bulb offshoots undisturbed for years. Bury the bulbs at least three times their height in the soil in the autumn.

Can also be grown from the seeds produced, but it is a long process, up to four years before they flower. Best to increase by splitting the bulbs in the autumn and replanting. Height 90–120 cm (3–4 ft); planting distance for bulbs about 23cm (9in).

Preparation
Cut when the flowers are nearly out, and hang upside down. If the heads 'fall' rather and lose their shape after a few days, prop them upright in a vase or jar in a warm place, and the heads should fall back into their round shape.

The results are equally effective if you wait until the seedheads have formed and pick then. Prop upright or hang.

A. sphaerocephalon should be picked before the flower heads open up.

ANAPHALIS
(pearl everlasting)

All species of anaphalis, which produce flat heads of closely packed white flowers, can be grown for drying. Most can be bought as plants from any nursery, and can be grown from seed.

Cultivation
Plant in the dormant season in a well-drained site, ordinary to poorish garden soil, in full sun or dry shade. The species *A. margaritacea* tends to spread rapidly by root; *A. triplinervis* is more compact in its habit. Height up to 45cm (18in); planting distance 38cm (15in).

Preparation
Cut when the flower heads are still tightly formed, strip off the leaves, and hang upside down. Once the tiny flowers which make up the clustered head start to open, the central part tends to become brown.

The heads do tend to stay floppy and droop even when quite dry, but can be supported by wiring, or the heads carefully propped up on stiffer material if necessary. The heads are especially useful, because they retain their milky whiteness, for using in flat, plate-like arrangements, when they can be chopped off from their stalks and used with 'fat' heads of other flowers, for example eryngiums, paeonias, etc.

AQUILEGIA VULGARIS (columbine, or granny's bonnet)

This columbine, with its flower heads like old bonnets, produces wonderful, elegant seedheads that dry well.

Cultivation

Can be grown quite easily from seed, planted in trays in the spring, and transplanted in late summer. Plants usually available from most nurseries. Plant out in sunny, or partially shaded position, in a moist soil. Height, up to 60cm (2ft); planting distance 30cm (1ft).

Preparation

Cut when the seedheads have just formed, and hang upside down or prop upright. Often the seedheads split immediately, sending a shower of tiny black seeds everywhere, so take precautions! Seedheads stay just as pretty when empty.

ARMERIA MARITIMA (thrift)

Neat tufts of stiff grass produce flower heads of round pink balls, which, bunched together, are ideal for making posies. Thrift can be grown from seed, sown in the spring, for planting out in the summer or autumn. Plants can often be bought from nurseries. Other types of armeria flowers can be dried, but avoid the smaller, rock garden species, which only grow a couple of fingers' height tall.

Cultivation

Plant in ordinary, well-drained garden soil, in full sun. Suitable for rock gardens, and tubs. Height about 30cm (1ft); planting distance the same.

Preparation

Cut as soon as the flowers emerge, and bunch together, before hanging upside down. Picking when the flowers are fully out usually means that they fade fast to a dull grey, and drop.

ARTEMISIA

A. absinthium 'Lambrook Silver' is one of the best of the artemisias to grow for drying, but most of the silver-leaved varieties dry well. It is one of the few foliages that does stay truly silvery-white, and contrasts well with spikes of copper-coloured docks or copper beech. Possible to grow from seed, but easily available from most nurseries, so hardly worth the trouble.

Cultivation

Plant in the dormant season in light well-drained soil and full sun. Height 90cm (3ft); planting distance 38cm (15in).

Preparation

Cut in full summer when the silver leaves are at their best, and before flowering. Strip off only a few inches from the base of the stem, and hang upside down.

ASTILBE X ARENDSII

This plant's plumes of pink and deep red flowers, and beautiful dissected leaves, can be dried and pressed. Usually readily available as plants from nurseries, the deeper pink-flowered varieties are more successful when used just for the drying of flowers.

Cultivation

Plant in moisture-retentive soil, in shady or partially shaded sites. Good plant for the edge of pools or small rivers. Plant during the dormant season. Height up to 90cm (3ft); planting distance 38cm (15in).

Preparation

Cut when the flowers are just up, before really opening out, and hang upside down. Dry fast. If unsuccessful in warm airing cupboard, then try in the oven, hanging upside down. Leave the oven door slightly ajar if they curl up too much (see p. 27 on oven drying).

The dark pink varieties turn even darker; the paler pinks and mid-pinks can often transform into apricot/tan colours. The very pale colours dry to dark cream/coffee colours. The leaves should be picked in early summer and pressed.

1 Aquilegia vulgaris
2 Armeria maritima
3 Artemisia absinthium
4 Astilbe x arendsii

1 Astrantia carniolica '*Rubra*'
2 Carlina acaulis
3 Catananche caerulea

ASTRANTIA
(masterwort)

A. carniolica, *A. major*, and *A. maxima*, all produce starry pale pink flowers, and white flowers tinged with pink, which dry well. Astrantias are available from most nurseries, but *A. carniolica* 'Rubra', a deeper pink one which is possibly the best to dry, may be more difficult to come by. It is still very beautiful when dried, and looks well in fat bunches. Not easy to raise from seed.

Cultivation
Plant in the dormant season in shade or partial shade, in a reasonably moist position. Full sun will also do, provided the soil stays reasonably moist. Height up to 60cm (2ft); planting distance 38cm (15in).

Preparation
Cut as soon as the flowers are nearly fully out, strip off the lower leaves and hang upside down. When dried, the flowers remain astonishingly true to their fresh counterparts.

ATHYRIUM FILIX-FEMINA
(lady fern)

All the varieties of this family press well. Obtainable from firms specializing in ferns. Ensure that all ferns ordered are hardy ones.

Cultivation
Plant in moisture-retentive soil, usually in a sheltered position. Height up to 90cm (3ft).

Preparation
Cut when the leaves have unfurled and are still very fresh and green. Cut from just above the soil level, strip off the lower leaves, and press.

BRIZA MEDIA
(quaking grass)

Succinctly named grass with slightly shiny, heart-shaped seedheads, which continue to rustle when dry; useful for small arrangements. Seed available from almost all seed merchants, although briza may be obtainable only within a packet containing other varieties of grass seeds for drying.

Cultivation
Easily grown from seed sown in the spring for planting out in the summer. Plant in well-drained soil in a sunny position. Height up to 45cm (18in); planting distance 15cm (6in). Spreads slowly by root.

Preparation
Cut as soon as the seedheads have formed. Cut from the base of the stem and hang upside down to dry, when they will gradually turn creamy gold.

CARLINA ACAULIS

Dramatic daisy-style flower, usually as big as the palm of a hand, which has a thistle-like consistency. The outer petals gleam gold/silver. One of the most spectacular flowers to dry, if slightly dependent on a good summer. Wonderful for making an impact in a large arrangement. Possible to grow from seed, although many do not ever germinate. Becoming more obtainable as a plant, especially by mail order or nurseries that buy from Holland.

Cultivation
Plant in ordinary, well-drained soil, in a very sunny position, as the flowers will not open unless there is considerable sunshine. Height,

up to 30cm (1ft); planting distance the same.

Preparation
Cut when the flowers are fully out on a reasonably sunny day. If picked when very wet, they can rot. Cut with as much stem as possible; leave on the thistle-like leaves, which dry well, and hang upside down to dry.

CATANANCHE
(Cupid's dart)

Why this flower acquired its common name is one of life's mysteries. *C. caerulea* has silver buds on the ends of bare stems. They are tightly clamped, and then suddenly open up to reveal indigo blue petals. Also available in lavender, white, and bicolour blue/white. If the blue can be preserved, and it certainly can, these are delightful flowers, which enhance other small-flowered species, such as *Lonas inodora*, helipterums, salvias, etc. It is fairly easy to buy as a plant from most nurseries. Seeds are available from more specialist seed merchants.

Cultivation
Sow the seeds under glass in spring for planting out in summer, and a chance of flowering the same year. Flowering will certainly take place the following year. Plant in ordinary soil, well drained, in a sunny position. Height 75cm (30in); planting distance 38cm (15in). The deep purple variety produces the best colour of flowers for drying.

Preparation
The challenge in cutting cupid's dart is to preserve the blue flowers. All too often the flowers are out, cutting takes place, and the

flowers fold up again, totally hiding the blue petals, and never open again. Trial and error reveals no logic in picking, but the longer the picking is delayed, the better the chance of preserving the petals. Hang upside down, and hope for the best.

CENTAUREA MACROCEPHALA

A relative of the cornflower family, *C. macrocephala* is a thistle-like flower, standing up to 1.5m (5ft) tall, with brilliant yellow tufts of petals. Easily grown from seed, it will generally flower the following year after planting. Seeds available from more specialist seed merchants.

Cultivation
Sow the seeds under glass in spring for planting out in late summer to early autumn. Needs a sunny, well-drained site, in ordinary garden soil. Height up to 1.5m (5ft); planting distance 60cm (2ft).

Preparation
Cut when the yellow flowers are totally out; strip off the leaves, leaving a manageable portion of stem (say 60cm [2ft]), and hang upside down.

These are fun to grow, and a splendid addition to any arrangement. One or two in an arrangement with other large flowers, such as carlinas, are very effective. If you miss drying the flowers at the right time, the seedhead shells dry well.

CORTADERIA SELLOANA (Pampas grass)

Silky white heads are redolent of unimaginative displays in bay windows or landings, plopped in a narrow-necked container and left for years. However, the heads can look marvellous as a foil for deep-coloured leaves such as copper beech. With the stems chopped off almost totally and used in arrangements with yellows and oranges, the effect is vibrant. Plants are obtainable from most nurseries, but as they increase abundantly, try acquiring a chunk from a friendly owner.

Cultivation
Plant in any well drained, sunny position. Beware the sharp leaves and use gloves for handling the plant or cutting. Most nurseries would advise a sheltered site, but pampas seems to survive happily in the fiercest of windy positions. Height up to 3m (9ft). Plant singly.

Preparation
Cut when the white plumes are just opening out and prop upright to dry, or hang upside down. Spray with hairspray to prevent dropping.

CROCOSMIA

Crocosmias are often confused with, and closely related to, montbretias. All species produce flowers in late summer with orange, yellow, or scarlet flowers. The most successful colours of flower for drying incline to the deep oranges and vivid scarlets. The deep red 'Lucifer' is excellent. Best to buy corms from nurseries; they are usually readily available.

Cultivation
Plant the corms in open sunny soil, which keeps damp in summer. Plant 5–7.5cm (2–3in) deep, 10cm (4in) apart. Height 75cm (30in).

Preparation
Cut when half the flowers are out, and at least half are still tightly shut. Hang upside down. Sometimes it is possible to cut the flowers at a much later stage and dry them, but occasionally the petals will fall. The flowers retain their colour well.

Owing to their spindly appearance, the flowers are most useful when they are hung in bunches, if possible all pointing in the same direction. In this way their vivid colouring has more impact.

CYNARA CARDUNCULUS (pink cardoon)

Impressive plant belonging to the same family as the artichoke, and with similar leaves. Produces thistle-like flowers with deep pink/purple tufts. Beloved of Victorian gardeners, but rarely seen now. A novelty to grow, and very easy to succeed from seed. The flowers are not quite as large and impressive as the plant would lead one to expect, but this is one of the few thistle-type flowers that can be dried. Easily grown from seed obtainable from more specialist seed merchants. Will often flower in first year.

Cultivation
Sow the seeds under glass in spring for planting out as soon as they are big enough (i.e. four leaves). Plant in a sunny or partially shaded site in ordinary garden soil. Planting early enough in the year will ensure that they flower the same year. Height 1.2–1.5m (4–5ft); planting distance 90cm (3ft).

Preparation
Cut from the base of the flower stem when the tufts of petals are well established. Picking too early

1 Centaurea macrocephala
2 *Crocosmia*
3 Cynara cardunculus
4 Delphinium elatum

3

2

4

1

5

1 Dianthus *x* allwoodi
2 Dianthus caryophyllus
3 *Dryopteris*
4 Echinops ritro
5 Eupatorium purpureum

will only cause the flower to shrivel without developing. Strip off the leaves and hang the stems upside down. The leaves press well.

DELPHINIUM

Few flower-driers can grow enough delphiniums; and such is their attraction that it is difficult to find the heart to cut them down when in flower. Plant some in an out-of-the-way area which is not a border, and the task is easier. Fairly easy to grow from seed, but readily available as a plant from most nurseries. *D. elatum* is the most popular species, although, like all delphiniums, it can be short lived. All colours, from the more familiar deep blues, to pink, lilac, and white, dry well.

These are worth growing for drying, especially for the wonderful blues. A flower which is often grown in public parks, etc.

Cultivation
Sow the seeds in spring for planting out in the summer. Plant bought plants during the dormant season in deep, rich soil, sheltered, and with a sunny position, where they can be left undisturbed for years. They may need staking during the flowering season. Height up to 1.5m (5ft); planting distance 45cm (18in).

Preparation
Cut when half the flowers on a stalk are out. Cut from the base of the stem, removing most of the leaves, and hang upside down to dry in the warmest heat possible. Only by fast drying is the colour retained, and the petals do not drop. The flower spike can be used whole, or easily trimmed of small florets for use in small arrangements.

DIANTHUS
(pinks and carnations)

Blue/green-leaved plant with highly-scented flowers, the double-flowered deeper rose pinks, reds, and whites of which dry well. Plants easily obtainable from most nurseries, but can be grown from seed available from most seed merchants. Double flowers tend to be more successful; beware of pale pinks, which can dry to a coffee cream. Old fashioned and modern pinks provide ideal flowers, the latter often perpetually flowering, and often in bloom until the first severe frost. The species *D. plumarius* often provides good flowers, easily grown from seeds.

Carnations bought in florists' shops, which are grown under glass, also provide ideal material to dry, if at more expense. But if a street market trader, for example, is selling off his carnations at low prices at the end of the day, this might provide much colour for arrangements over many months, and therefore good value.

Cultivation
Sow seeds under glass in spring for planting out in the summer. Plant in a sunny, well-drained site. Ideal for rockeries or tubs, depending on the height of the particular flower. Height from 15–60cm (6–24in). Often a short-lived perennial, and therefore advisable to take cuttings during the summer for new plants. To ensure good flowers, pick off the central flower stem to encourage good side shoots.

Preparation
Cut when the flowers are nearly out, and hang upside down to dry. The stems dry very well, as does the foliage, so retain leaves near the top of the stem.

ECHINOPS
(globe thistle)

E. banaticus and *E. ritro* both produce globular flowers in steely blue or white. Their metallic sheen goes well with all other blue and deep pink materials. The species *E. ritro* is easier to come by than *E. banaticus*, and is available from most nurseries. Growing from seed is fairly easy, and seeds are available from more specialist seed merchants.

Cultivation
Sow seeds under glass in spring for planting out in the summer, or put purchased plants in the ground during the dormant season. Echinops need a sunny position, in well-drained soil, and generally form large clumps without too much difficulty. Height around 1.2m (4ft); planting distance 60cm (2ft).

Preparation
Cut when the round flowers are just coming out, and hang upside down. Too much rain, or leaving picking a little late, can lead to the thistle-like heads splitting and dropping. If you think this is about to happen, try salvaging by spraying with hair lacquer.

ERICA
(heaths and heathers)

Heather and heath flowers dry so well they are almost indistinguishable from the fresh plant. Pure whites, deep pinks, and purples of the smaller-flowered varieties dry best. Plants are so easily obtainable that there is no point in trying to grow from seeds or cuttings.

Heathers are overlooked now as a dried flower, but, used on their own, or in bunches with other material in a small arrangement, are very effective.

Cultivation

Ideally they should be planted in a peaty, acidic soil, although they will thrive in many other types. Contrary to popular myth, ericas do not like being planted in pure peat. Plant at any time during the year except during a hard frost or midsummer, in a damp spot, with sun or partial shade.

Preparation

Cut when the flower spikes are out half-way up the stem. Cut from the base of the stems and hang upside down to dry. During a dry period, the flowers may drop.

The time-honoured way of preserving heather in Scotland is to stab holes in a fresh potato with a skewer, and insert the heather stalks, building up with more and more material until the potato can hardly be seen.

ERYNGIUM

Several varieties of this blue thistle flower are available. The more popular ones are easily obtainable from nurseries, others from more specialist dealers. Possible to grow from seed; germination usually takes place within a couple of months. Sow in early spring under glass, transplanting out in late summer to early autumn.

E. alpinum is a smaller version, *E. x oliverianum* and *E. alpinum* are the best known, and *E. maritimum* is more greeny-blue. *E. giganteum*, which includes 'Miss Wilmott's ghost' (illustrated opposite) is more ivory-blue, and does fade a little when dry.

The smaller varieties, such as *E. alpinum* produce more flowers per stem. The larger versions, such as *E. giganteum* and *E. maritimum*, are large and rather prickly specimens with which to deal, but look magnificent combined with delphiniums, euphorbias, and pressed ferns or bamboo.

Cultivation

Plant in ordinary garden soil, in a sunny and well-drained site, and if possible in a fairly sheltered position, as the flowers tend to fall over in rain or strong winds. Plant out purchased plants during the dormant season. Height from 60–120cm (2–4ft); planting distance the same.

Preparation

Cut when the flowers are nearly out, and hang upside down, removing only the lower leaves, as they do dry well and frame the flowers attractively. If the outer flower petals continually close up, then chop all but a short stem (which can be wired later) and place the flower upside down on chicken wire/wire cake-tray, etc. to dry.

Despite the possibility of fading, the intriguing shapes remain interesting for many months. If they do fade too fast, spraying very lightly with car sprays in greens and blues will have a magical effect.

EUPATORIUM
(hemp agrimony)

Eupatoriums are large plants, ideal for wild gardens or the backs of borders, which readily produce pinky-silver flowers up to 15cm (6in) across. *E. cannabinum* and *E. purpureum* can be available as plants from more specialist nurseries. Once established, eupatoriums produce many flowers for your money!

Cultivation

Plant in sun or shaded spot with soil that will remain moist, allowing plenty of room for growth, as *E. purpureum* can reach 1.8m (6ft), while *E. cannabinum* grows to 1.2m (4ft).

Preparation

Cut when the flowers are well formed, leaving on 60cm (2ft) of stem, and place the stalk in foam, drying the flower upright. The tiny pink inside flowers may drop out, leaving the silver flower 'containers' only. Both appearances are equally pretty. The large flower heads can be divided to make them more manageable, although using them whole is effective, for example, as a lacy fringe round a fairly solid arrangement of greenery, hydrangeas etc.

EUPHORBIA

E. robbiae and *E. wulfenii*, which both have yellow/lime green foliage and flowers, dry very well, and maintain their clean colours for a long time when dried. Their fresh green is wonderful for adding to any arrangement. *E. polychroma*, with its yellow/lime green bracts which eventually turn to red, also dries quite well at the early stage, or when just showing tints of red. Possible to grow from seeds obtainable from more specialist seed merchants. Plants available from more specialist nurseries, but, owing to their increasing popularity, search the local nursery first.

Cultivation

Sow the seeds under glass in spring for planting out in the late summer or autumn. Plant purchased specimens during the dormant season, in a sunny, open site.

3

2

5

1 *Erica*
2 Eryngium alpinum
3 Eryngium giganteum
4 *Euphorbia*
5 *Gnaphalium*

4

I

1 *Heuchera*
2 Hosta fortunei
3 Iris foetidissima
4 Liatris spicata

E. wulfenii, which grows to 1.2m (4ft), should be planted near a wall to gain shelter. *E. robbiae* reaches 45cm (18in); planting distance 60cm (2ft).

Preparation

Cut when the flowers are nearly fully out, and hang upside down. Beware the juice from the freshly cut stems that can irritate sensitive skin, especially when exposed to sunlight.

GNAPHALIUM

Related to the helichrysum genus, this white-grey felty-leaved plant, with clear lemon-yellow clusters of tiny flowers, is easily grown from seed, obtainable from more specialist seed merchants.

Cultivation

Sow seeds under glass in early spring, planting out in late spring or early summer in a very sunny, well-drained site. Good as a rockery or planted for tubs. Can flower the same year as sowing. Height 15cm (6in); planting distance the same.

Preparation

Cut when the tightly-clustered flowers show touches of yellow, but before the centre of any tiny flower opens up to reveal a mustard yellow/orange centre. Hang upside down. Bunches of gnaphalium can be used combined with lavender, lonas, polygonum, and small roses for tiny arrangements.

GYPSOPHILA

Clouds of white miniature flowers emerge from *G. paniculata* (baby's breath), which is the most useful of the varieties to grow; a few well-established plants will produce an astonishing number of flowers.

Easy to grow from seed, obtainable from most seed merchants. Roots available from many of the mail order catalogues from Holland. The double-flowered variety is best.

Cultivation

Plant in an open, sunny site, where the flowers, which do not often appear until late summer/early autumn, are not subject to early frosts. Beware of slugs, which eat the emerging shoots and can cause the sudden disappearance of the plant in early summer. Height up to 90cm (3ft); planting distance the same.

Preparation

Cut when the tiny flowers are fully out, and hang upside down. The stems can be broken up for small arrangements, or left *en masse* and inserted into an unusual bowl.

HEUCHERA

Tough plants with attractive leaves and stems covered with tiny branches of coral pink or red flowers. Not always successful as a dried flower, because the colour tends to darken. Readily available from most nurseries.

Cultivation

Plant in walls, under deciduous trees, or shrubs, in a sunny or partially shaded position. Divide every other year in the autumn. Height up to 45cm (18in); planting distance the same.

Preparation

Cut when the flowers are just opening out, and hang upside down. Try them as a massed arrangement, possibly sprayed with gold or silver.

HOSTA
(plantain lily)

Primarily grown for their leaves, which are slightly floppy, but wonderful edging material for posies and small arrangements, Hostas are readily available at most nurseries. The leaves dry very well by pressing, and the most successful varieties are those such as *H. fortunei* and *H. crispula*, with variegated leaves. The more fleshy-leaved *H. sieboldiana* does not press well.

Cultivation

Plant in moisture-retentive ordinary garden soil, in sun or shade. During wet spells protect from slugs, which love the leaves. Height up to 30cm (1ft); planting distance the same.

Preparation

Cut during the summer, when the leaves are well formed, taking care to pick from the base of the leaf, when there is as little moisture as possible. Pick only perfect leaves. Spots and small holes on hostas appear to be magnified considerably when dried.

IRIS FOETIDISSIMA
(stinking iris)

This species of iris produces gleaming orange seedheads in the autumn after the rather insignificant flowers. Almost unique in the dried flower annals, the shiny seeds give life to all sorts of arrangements, and can look spectacular mixed with all the other 'hot' colours of coppers, deep red, maroons, and oranges. Corms obtainable from more specialist nurseries. The common name derives from the leaves, which throw out an unattractive smell when bruised.

Cultivation

Plant in open, rich, well-drained soil in a sunny or slightly shaded position. Irises hate to be water-logged at any time. Height 50cm (20in); planting distance about 45cm (18in). Plant the corms 5cm (2in) deep. Can be slow growing.

Preparation

Cut when the seedpods have split open to reveal the seeds inside, and hang upside down or stand in a block of foam to dry. Often best to spray to prevent seeds dropping.

LIATRIS
(blazing star)

L. spicata has spikes of flowers that come in bright magenta purple, white, or dark purple, and which open from the top downwards on the stem. Can be grown from seeds which are available from most seed merchants, but will rarely flower until the third year. Unlike the species *L. callilepis*, which thrives on poor soil, *L. spicata* likes bogs, or waterside locations. Plants sometimes available at nurseries.

Cultivation

Sow from seed in early spring under glass, planting out in the late summer or autumn, or put purchased plants in the correct site during the dormant season. Liatris like an open, sunny position, with a moist soil. Height up to 90cm (3ft); planting distance 45cm (18in).

Preparation

Cut when the petals are opening up half-way down the flower stem, and hang upside down.

LIMONIUM
(sea lavender)

L. incanum dumosum, and *L. latifolium* both produce clouds of tiny rose, lavender, or silver-white flowers. Both varieties can easily be grown from seed, obtainable from more specialist seed merchants.

Tricky to grow in northern and windy areas, but rewarding with masses of flowers in a good summer. Fairly cheap to buy Holland-grown flowers in the late autumn, so it is a good idea to boost stocks in this way after a poor summer's crop.

Cultivation

Sow the seeds in spring under glass, transplanting out in the sunniest, most sheltered spot possible in ordinary well-drained garden soil in autumn. Should flower in a year, but prone to dislike a late spring, and flowering can be erratic. Height up to 60cm (2ft); planting distance 38cm (15in).

Preparation

Cut when the flowers have fully formed, and hang upside down. Picking early does not guarantee that the flowers will open fully.

LUPINUS POLYPHYLLUS
(lupin)

This popular lupin produces flowers in a multitude of colours. The individual seedheads are excellent for filling in tiny posies. Can easily be grown from seed, or purchased from nurseries. Often fairly short lived.

Cultivation

Sow seeds in early spring for planting out in late summer/early autumn. They will thrive for only short periods on heavy clay soils. Plant in sun, or partial shade. Height up to 1.2m (4ft); planting distance 60cm (2ft).

Preparation

Cut the greyish seedheads when they are just formed, even if this means cutting the whole flower spike with the odd flower still out at the top. Not only do the seedheads dry very well, but this prompt cutting will possibly ensure a good succession of blooms. Prop upright or hang upside down in fairly warm conditions; if necessary use hair lacquer to ensure the pods do not open and scatter seeds.

PAEONIA
(paeony, or peony)

Double paeony flowers of nearly all colours dry well; colours which are best for drying tend to be the mid to deep pinks. Deep red tends to turn very dark. The leaves are outstanding for pressing, provided you can ensure that they are really dry.

P. lactiflora and *P. officinalis* are the most commonly grown, and are easily available to buy from nurseries.

Cultivation

Plant in moist, richly prepared garden soil, in sun or partial shade, if possible where they will receive a little shelter, or where they can easily be reached for staking. Being an early flowering summer plant, they often receive late spring winds, and the heavy heads are dashed to the ground. Very long-lived plants, so should be settled into a patch for life! Height up to 60cm (2ft); planting distance 90cm (3ft).

1 Limonium latifolium
2 Lupinus polyphyllus
3 *Paeonia*
4 Polygonum bistorta

Preparation

Cut when the flowers are just emerging from bud form, splitting to show a glint of colour. Pick with 30cm (1ft), or so of stem, strip off the lower leaves, and hang upside down in fast heat, in the warmest place in the house. The only difficulty is in making sure that the flowers are dry and at the perfect time to pick: too wet or too open, and they rot and fall.

The wonderful leaves of all paeonies can be pressed; you can pick them during the summer when they are green, or wait until the early autumn, when they are tinged with deep reds, and press when the leaves are at their driest to preserve this colour. They can be used whole or in small sections.

PHYSALIS ALKEKENGI (Chinese lanterns)

This uninteresting plant with dull white flowers transforms later with glowing fireglow orange lanterns, which are really the calyx which surrounds the fruit. Can be grown from seed, but plants can often be obtained from nurseries. As it is a 'fast-creeping root plant', any garden with a good show might be more than happy to give away a few roots.

Yvonne Mallet, who produced the arrangements for this book, once made a forest of Chinese lantern trees. She hang-dried a dozen small silver birch trees until they lost their leaves, and planted each one in a container. She then stuck on dozens of Chinese lanterns with a hot glue gun, either still closed, or cut open via their petal edges to appear as flowers. This was to decorate a huge, cavernous interior for a charity ball; but the idea of using the lanterns

in the same way could be copied to more modest effect.

Cultivation

Sow the seeds under glass in early spring, uncovered, as they need light to germinate, transplanting to the flowering site in early autumn. Plant purchased plants during dormant period in sunny, well-drained soil where they can be controlled, e.g. with a wall to at least one side. Height up to 60cm (2ft); planting distance the same.

Preparation

Cut when the orange colour appears in the majority of the lanterns. Chop off from the base, strip off all leaves, and hang or prop upright to dry.

POLYGONUM (knotweed)

P. affine and *P. bistorta* 'Superbum' are root-spreading plants which produce spikes of deep pink flowers in summer onwards. *P. baldschuanicum* is the 'mile-a-minute' Russian vine, really only to be planted if you have an eyesore to cover, or a neighbour to block out. It can grow up to 9m (30ft) a year and needs much pruning to keep it in check. It produces hanging chandelier-type flowers which dry well. But the plant is a substantial commitment! Best to pick the flowers if one is already in existence than to plant specially.

Cultivation

Plants are usually readily available from nurseries. Try, if possible, to choose a *P. affine* or *P. bistorta* which produces deep pink flowers, as these dry best. Plant in ordinary soil, sun or light shade. Height up to 38cm (15in); planting distance the same.

Preparation

Cut when the flowers are well formed, and bunch together. Hang upside down.

PULMONARIA (lungwort, soldiers and sailors)

Spot-leaved ground cover plant with blue and pink flowers in the spring. Plants of both *P. officinalis*, with spotted leaves, and *P. saccharata*, with blotched silvery leaves, are readily available from most nurseries. Wonderful value for framing and surrounding small posies, their green colour preserves well for up to a year.

Cultivation

Plant in a partially shaded position with moist ordinary garden soil. Height up to 30cm (1ft); planting distance the same.

Preparation

Cut just after the flowers have died in late spring; the leaves will have increased in size, and are at their best. Cut off from the base of the stem and press. Pick only perfect leaves, as the slightest blemish seems to magnify to a large brown spot when dry.

SANTOLINA CHAMAECYPARISSUS (cotton lavender)

An aromatic, silver, feathery-leaved plant which produces round, pompon, bright yellow flowers. Plants readily available from most nurseries or herb growers.

Cultivation

Plant during the dormant season in full sun, in ordinary, well-drained garden soil. Chopping off flower heads regularly will ensure a long flowering season. Height 60cm (2ft); planting distance the same.

Preparation

Cut from the base of the branch when the flowers are nearly fully out, and hang upside down. The foliage dries very well, so resist stripping off more leaves than necessary. The scent remains for months, and a bowl of cotton lavender mixed with other white and yellow flowers looks and smells fresh.

SENECIO

S. *laxifolius*, or S. *greyi* (plants listed under this name are invariably S. *laxifolius*), has distinct green leaves with silvery-grey undersides, and yellow daisy-like flowers. The flowers dry well, despite closing up, and the leaves press or hang-dry. Plants available from most nurseries.

Cultivation

Plant during the dormant season in a sunny, well-drained site, ordinary garden soil. Senecios like coastal areas. Height about 1.2m (4ft); planting distance 90cm (3ft).

Preparation

Cut when the flowers are nearly out, stripping off any leaves, and hang upside down. Small-leaved branches can be hung, but probably do better pressed.

SOLIDAGO
(golden rod)

Feathery plumes of fluffy yellow flowers, sometimes reaching 1.5–1.8m (5–6ft), can make solidago a rather overwhelming plant, especially as it is very greedy, and will need to be divided and replanted every other year. It is

better to buy dwarf varieties of the many garden hybrids, such as 'Lemore', which is pale primrose yellow, height 60cm (2ft), or 'Goldenmosa', which has sprays of fluffy flowers, is readily available from most nurseries. The gulf in quality between these and the common garden forms is immense, so it is worth searching for interesting species.

Cultivation

Plant in enriched garden soil, in full sun or light shade. Height and planting distance conditional on type.

Preparation

Cut when the flowers are nearly showing yellow, almost before the tips have coloured. Leave on the leaves near the flower spike, stripping only from the base of the stalk. Do not be tempted to cut later, as inevitably the flowers will turn an uninteresting pale straw colour.

STACHYS LANATA
(lamb's tongue)

S. *lanata* produces spikes of silvery-grey, heavily-felted flowers, pierced with tiny deep mauve petals. Spreads readily from a root. Plants available from any nursery. Be sure not to buy the 'Silver Carpet' variety, which has identical leaves, but no flowers.

Beth Chatto (see *Suppliers* on p. 123) has one called S. *olympica* 'Cotton Boll', which has round, bobble, cotton-wool type flowers, and when dry is far less brittle than the usual types.

Cultivation

Plant in a well-drained sunny site. *Stachys lanata* will tolerate almost any soil except one which becomes

readily waterlogged. Height up to 45cm (18in); planting distance 30cm (1ft) or less if you want a dense ground-cover effect.

Preparation

Cut when the flower spikes have formed, and just when a twinkling of the mauve flowers is visible. Cut from the base of the stem (there is no need to strip leaves), and hang upside down (which will produce fairly straight plants) or prop upright (which will cause the heads to droop over attractively at the top).

VERBASCUM BOMBYCIFERUM
(mullein)

This biennial has large felty grey-green leaves and a few spikes of silvery pods which open out to yellow flowers. Obtainable from more specialist seed merchants.

Cultivation

Sow seeds in summer, for planting in permanent site, in ordinary soil and full sun, in autumn. Height up to 1.8m (6ft); planting distance 60cm (2ft).

Preparation

Cut when the flower spikes have a good smattering of flowers out. Hang upside down.

Sometimes this plant can dry very well indeed, and therefore provides a spectacular addition for a tall arrangement. At other times, drying can produce only a very dull grey seedhead, which can be vastly improved with some judicious silver spraying. I love it for the unexpected shapes, and would always find room for a couple, if only for novelty value.

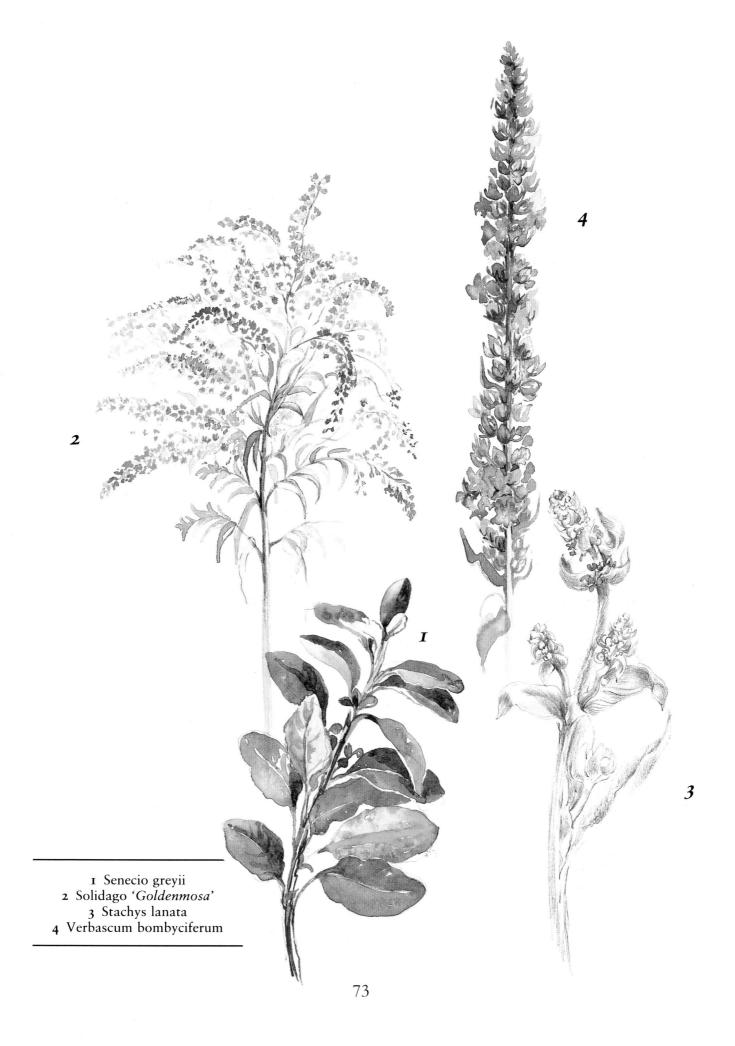

1 Senecio greyii
2 Solidago 'Goldenmosa'
3 Stachys lanata
4 Verbascum bombyciferum

SHRUBS AND TREES

Many of the shrubs and trees in this group are unsuitable to plant in a small garden. Many can be found in large public open spaces and in the countryside.

ACER
(maple)

Leaves and small branches of nearly all varieties of maples, whether green or in reddish autumnal colours, press well. The most popular for planting in gardens are the slow-growing *A. japonicum* and *A. palmatum* (Japanese maple). Never be tempted to plant the common sycamore, *A. pseudoplatanus*, which produces thousands of wind-borne flying seeds, which settle and seed themselves prolifically.

Cultivation
Acers can be bought from most nurseries, and should be planted in neutral to acidic soil, in a sunny, or lightly shaded position, with some shelter.

Preparation
Cut the leaves at any time after they are fully mature, either when green or later in autumnal colours. Search for wild sycamore and cut them in summer, as the leaves rarely turn the interesting colours of the cultivated versions. Wire if necessary.

ARUNDINARIA
(bamboo)

Several bamboos survive happily in Britain. *A. japonica* and *A. nitida* are too fast-growing and spreading for smaller gardens; *A. murielae* is more suitable. One of the easiest of greenery to dry, its waving thread-like leaves are wonderful additions to arrangements. Plants available from more specialist nurseries.

Cultivation
Plant in ordinary, moist garden soil; *A. nitida* will be more at home in shade than the others, which prefer sunshine. Height: *A. japonica* and *A. nitida* will reach at least 3m (10ft); *A. murielae* will touch only 2.4m (8ft).

Preparation
Cut when the fresh green leaves appear in the spring or summer, though picking and drying later is also successful. Hang-dry fairly quickly, in the warmest place in the house.

BALLOTA PSEUDODICTAMNUS

This fairly hardy shrub has felty, grey-green rounded leaves which dry well. The unusual, almost pale grey/lime green colouring makes this a very useful filler in arrangements. Obtainable from more specialist nurseries.

Cultivation
Plant in well-drained, ordinary soil in full sun. Beware of allowing it to become too wet, as ballotas tend to rot; otherwise they are easy to cultivate. Height 60cm (2ft).

Preparation
Cut during the early summer when the leaves are well formed, strip off lower leaves, and either hang upside down or stab into foam and leave to dry.

BUDDLEIA DAVIDII
(butterfly bush)

B. davidii, which is the fast-growing and most popularly grown buddleia, produces large, dense seedheads, which can be dried when green. The large-flowered pure white varieties, such as 'White Cloud' or 'White Profusion', seem the best. Obtainable from most nurseries.

Cultivation
Plant in full sun, ordinary garden soil. To produce the maximum flush of flowers, cut down to within 1.2–1.5m (4–5ft) of the ground in the early autumn, or before there is too much danger of hard frost. Alternatively, leave cutting until the early spring. Height up to 2.7m (9ft).

Preparation
Cut when the seedpods have just formed, and hang upside down. If the seeds do start to loosen, then firm with hair lacquer.

BUXUS SEMPERVIRENS
(box)

This slow-growing common box preserves well and is obtainable from most nurseries.

Cultivation
Plant in any good garden soil, in sun or shade. Height up to 3m (10ft), but it is normally grown as a hedge of only 60cm (2ft) tall.

Preparation
Cut at any time but best in midsummer, when the growth is still spurting. Any spaces will quickly be refilled. Cut off small

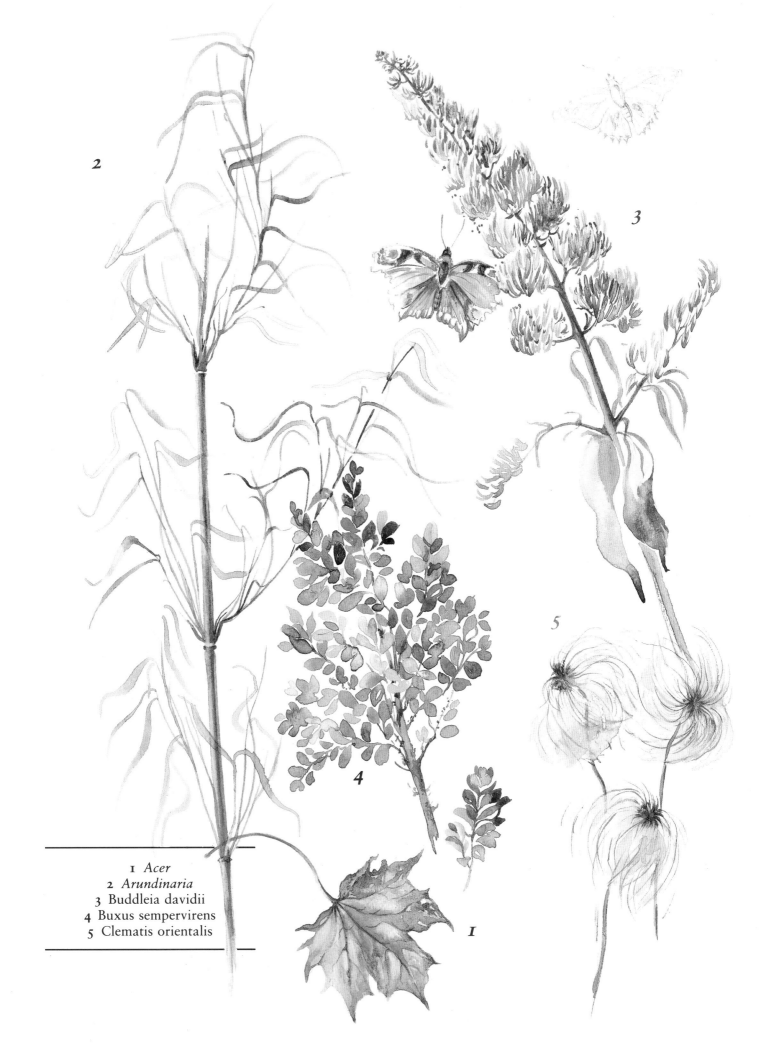

1 *Acer*
2 *Arundinaria*
3 Buddleia davidii
4 Buxus sempervirens
5 Clematis orientalis

1 Cotoneaster horizontalis
2 Eucalyptus gunni
3 Fagus sylvatica 'Cuprea'
4 Garrya elliptica
5 Ilex

branches (a hedge which has been trimmed for years will have a very tough lower branch), and dry by hanging upside down. Will remain green.

CLEMATIS

C. orientalis, and *C. tangutica*, both vigorous climbers with bright yellow flowers, produce feathery wispy seedheads for drying. Available from more specialist nurseries.

Cultivation
Plant so that the roots are in moist shade, if possible, and where the plant can be allowed to ramble freely upwards. The flowers are best seen from below. Height up to 7.5m (25ft).

Preparation
Cut when the seedheads have formed, with 2.5–5cm (1–2in) of stem. They can be made into small bunches and hung upside down, but it is often easier to stick the stalks into a block of foam. To be on the safe side, spray with hair lacquer to prevent them disintegrating.

COTONEASTER HORIZONTALIS

This deciduous shrub grows in a fan shape, outwards into paths or up walls, and before the berries emerge it is ideal for pressing. Obtainable from most nurseries.

Cultivation
Plant in ordinary to poor garden soil, or at the edge of gravel paths. It prefers a sunny position, but survives quite happily in partial or almost total shade; will spread to almost 2.4m (8ft) if left unchecked.

Preparation
Cut when the leaves are well formed in the midsummer, chopping about half-way down a branch, which will soon heal over. Make sure that you do this well before the berries emerge, as they will not press well!

EUCALYPTUS GUNNII
(gum tree)

The young blue-green branches and leaves of eucalyptus preserve perfectly by hanging, or propping upright. *E. gunnii* is reasonably hardy in Britain, and is available from most nurseries.

Cultivation
Plant in a sheltered site, neutral to acidic soil, where they can have maximum sunlight. Stake firmly and ensure that they do not dry out in the first few years. Height up to 7.5m (25ft); after the first few years growth is very rapid. Keep cutting back to ensure that the attractive, young leaves, which are the best ones for drying, keep sprouting continuously.

Preparation
Cut the young, rounded-leaved branches, up to 60cm (2ft) long, during the summer. They can be hung upside down to dry, but I found that placing them in slightly damp foam in a warm place, and leaving for a few weeks until they had totally dried, left the leaves looking almost identical to the fresh tree. (Placing the small branches in an arrangement after giving them a soak for a day or so may well achieve the same result.) When hung-dry, the leaves tend to fold in slightly.

FAGUS SYLVATICA 'CUPREA'
(copper beech)

Copper beech is not a tree to be planted in most gardens, as it can attain a height of 12m (40ft). Grown as a hedge, however, it is controllable, and effective as a screen for the summer, autumn and much of the winter, as the old leaves tend to hang on until replaced in the spring.

Copper beech supports all the 'hot' colours superbly: terracotta and orange helichrysums, the oranges of physalis (Chinese lanterns), and crocosmia, and shows up clearly many golden grasses.

Cultivation
Plant 45cm (18in) plants about the same distance apart for hedging. Thrives on any soil except heavy clay.

Preparation
Cut when the leaves are well established, in early summer. Press small branches, about 60cm (2ft) long, in a fan shape, trimming out leaves that would overlap. Contrary to the belief that copper beech does well only when preserved with glycerine, this method is very effective, although the leaves don't retain the same depth of colour as when glycerined.

GARRYA ELLIPTICA

This quick-growing shrub is chosen for its decorative hanging catkins, which emerge in the very early spring but often appear in late autumn. The male plants have longer catkins than the females, but both produce the catkins without the benefit of the other, although to bear fruit, they must cross-pollinate. Available from more specialist nurseries.

Cultivation
Buy pot-grown plants, as they resent root disturbance, and plant in a well-drained site, with shelter from the prevailing or sea-borne winds. Height up to 4.5m (15ft); spread about 2.7m (9ft).

Preparation
Cut whenever the catkins are still tightly formed, fairly soon after they emerge. Later, when they dangle down in profusion, they do not dry quite as well. Choose a few small branches, no more than 15cm (6in) long, which can be propped upright in a container in a very warm place, or hung upside down. The small branches can be stuck at an angle into arrangements, when the catkins will droop and shiver in slight breezes. Catkins picked early usually stay supple.

HEDERA
(ivy)

Many ivies press well, from the ordinary wild type to all sorts of variegated species. Try any that come to hand. Picking the creamy or white-marked ones early in the season will ensure that they retain their colours. Later, or after prolonged rain, they tend to become brown rather fast.

Cultivation
Plant in any ordinary garden soil, in any position, shade or sunlight, where they can readily climb. Few need any support.

Preparation
Cut when the leaves are still growing fast, in the early summer, picking off attractive curving pieces; and, making sure that the leaves do not overlap, try to press in the same curving shapes. Ivies are wonderful for training down from the front of an arrangement, or for spraying with bronze, gold, or silver for Christmas.

HYDRANGEA

One of the stars of flowers for drying, many varieties of hydrangeas can be dried. *H. macrophylla*, *H. paniculata*, and *H. petiolaris* can readily be bought at any nursery.

Cultivation
Plant in good, rich, moisture-retentive soil. For both *H. macrophylla* and *H. paniculata* choose a sheltered position, either next to a wall or relatively close to established trees for protection from early frosts. *H. petiolaris* is a climbing species that grows well up a north or shaded wall, and can reach a height of 9m (30ft).

Preparation
Much advice and myth abounds about successful preserving of hydrangeas. The following is simple and almost foolproof.

Pick the flowers of *H. macrophylla* with about 10cm (4in) of stem left (cutting off too much means that next year's flowering stem is lost). Do this when the central floret within each flower is beginning to wither and the flower petals feel leathery; picking too early means that the flowers will shrivel. If in any doubt, place the flower stems in an inch or so of water, and leave in a warm place. The water will be absorbed and the head will mature, starting to dry at the same time, and can just be left upright to finish drying.

H. paniculata is easier to judge.

Pick with a 12.5cm (5in) of stem, only when fully out. Leave upright in a small amount of water until totally dry. It rarely fails to dry well.

H. petiolaris should be picked with no more than 15cm (6in) of stem when the outer petals have turned from white to greeny white, and the heads incline outwards and downwards. Dry by hanging upside down. Rarely poses problems.

If you have hydrangeas, then the problems are minimal, as picking is virtually at the end of the season, so the garden suffers little loss. For those without, beg from gardens that have the flowers in abundance!

H. macrophylla can be used whole, or easily broken up into smaller segments; deep pink, maroon, or blue dry well. *H. paniculata* stays the same fresh creamy pink, and white, and both it and *H. petiolaris* look spectacular in copper or brass containers, against dark woods or walls, where their petals and colours show up.

ILEX
(holly)

Most hollies can be dried successfully, with the berries shrivelling but drying brightly coloured on the stem. The variegated types do not dry as well as the all-green-leaved species, the leaves of which turn a pale, very pretty olive green. Hollies are obtainable from most nurseries.

Cultivation
Plant in sun or shade in ordinary but moist garden soil.

Preparation
Cut when the berries are well

1 *Hedera*
2 Hydrangea macrophylla
3 Hydrangea paniculata
4 Hydrangea petiolaris

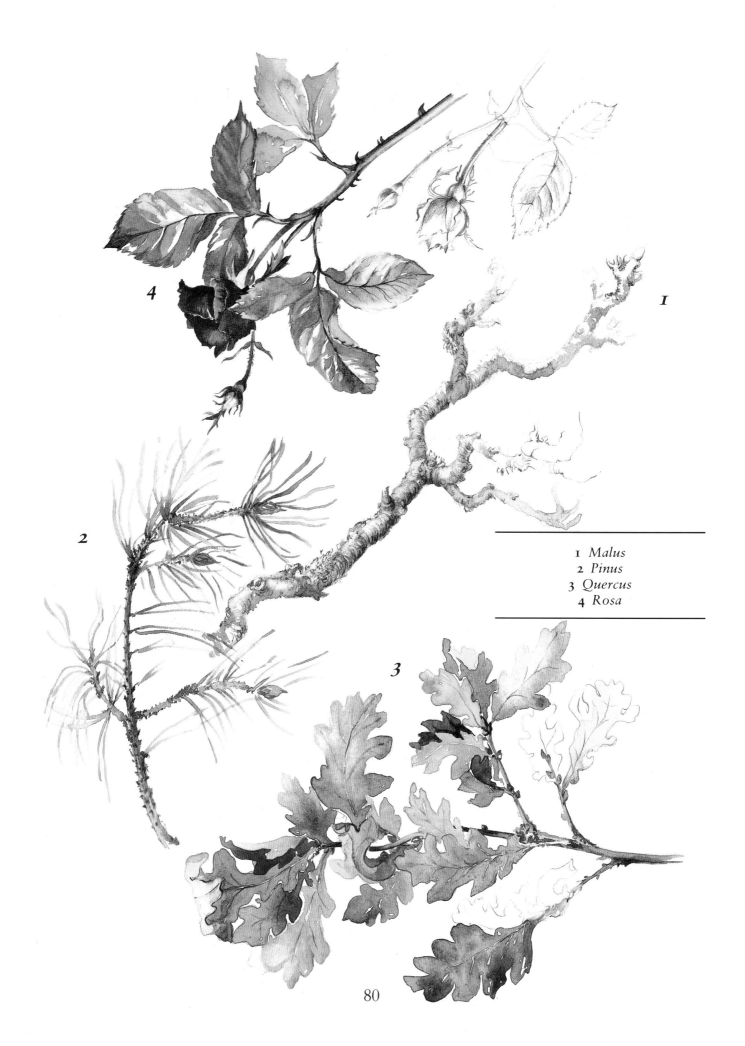

1 *Malus*
2 *Pinus*
3 *Quercus*
4 *Rosa*

80

formed, which is usually in the autumn, snipping off small branches and hanging them upside down in fast heat, such as a very warm airing cupboard.

MALUS SYLVESTRIS
(apple)

No need to buy an apple tree for this, as this only really works with older trees. The older and more gnarled the tree, the better, and the more it needs pruning, even better. If it has a good covering of lichen, better still. Choose your own tree, or look out for old orchards that need pruning, ruined cottages that still have a few ancient fruit trees growing, or just ask the neighbours.

Preparation

Cut off the top section of a crossing, or ingrowing, branch during the later autumn or on a mild winter day. Make sure that this branch is from the centre of the tree. (Apple trees should always be pruned so that the central part allows in much light for good growth, so you will be doing the tree a power of good.) Make a clean cut with a large pair of secateurs or a small saw of 90cm (3ft) of twisted branch. There is no need to dry the branch, as such; by the spring time, it will be lifeless and no leaves will sprout.

Sink the branches in cement or sand, or just jam them into a container that is weighted down; either cover the ends of the branches with foam into which you can stick flowers, or simply glue flowers directly onto the wood.

PINUS SYLVESTRIS
(Scots pine)

P. sylvestris will dry perfectly, complete with small cones. If you think that the needles might fall, remembering the mess of a dry Christmas tree, then the spray sold for Christmas trees to help them retain their needles should be applied, and all will be well. Not a tree for a small garden.

Preparation

Cut small branches, no more than 30cm (1ft) long in late summer, complete with small cones if possible, and hang upside down somewhere where they can dry quickly.

QUERCUS ROBUR
(oak)

Q. robur (formerly *Q. pedunculata*) is the age-old common or English oak. Small oak branches preserve beautifully by pressing.

Preparation

Cut 60cm (2ft) lengths during the summer, and remove overlapping leaves before pressing. Better to remove more leaves, and dry a sparse branch, than have a thick wadge of leaves. The wavy edges to the leaves look charming in any setting.

ROSA
(rose)

Roses of many hues and types can be dried. Everyone has their favourites and thinks that only certain types will dry successfully, and they are probably right: it is the right rose to dry in their area and conditions.

I have tried drying many types, and there are but a few which will not dry, such as very pale yellows and pinks, and the multicolours, pinks and yellows, but many more which are very successful. The small double-flowered floribundas are often the most successful; try 'Dorothy Perkins' (both pale and dark pink); 'Fairy'; 'Coral Cluster'; 'Phyllis Bide'; 'Pink Grootendorst' (wonderful colour, dries beautifully but very prickly); 'Paul Crampel', and 'Golden Salmon Superieur'. The hybrid teas are also worth trying.

I started several years ago by simply drying all the buds I was cutting down during the autumn pruning. Astonishingly, 'Iceberg', the modern floribunda, dries prettily, looking like a faded Victorian wedding posy. Dark reds do tend to become maroon, the rather lax floribundas such as 'Queen Elizabeth' tend to drop, and the 'old' roses with their one flowering season, sweet scents, and glorious double flower heads do not really dry at all.

Preparation

It does seem to be important to pick after several dry days. Pick when the buds are well formed, but before any are open, and, stripping off the lower leaves, dry upside down in the warmest, driest heat you have (bar an oven, which does not seem to work).

It is convenient to pick off the bud with only a finger's length of stalk, and dry; it can be wired later.

Preserving roses does seem to be the ultimate in cheating nature and bringing the summer into the house for the whole year. Whole bunches of roses together, even mixed with just ferns for greenery and the odd piece of gypsophila, work wonders for morale in mid-February!

WILD PLANTS AND HERBS

ACHILLEA MILLEFOLIUM (yarrow)

Flat-topped flowers contain masses of tiny pink or white flowers. Aromatic leaves.

Habitat
Edges of roads in open, grassy turf. Meadows and verges where soil is reasonably nutritious.

Height
Up to 50cm (20in).

Preparation
When the flowers are fully out, strip off any leaves and hang upside down. After rain, they may turn brown when dry, in which case discard.

Achillea millefolium

ALISMA PLANTAGO AQUATICA (water plantain)

Airy-looking plant with pale-pink flower heads which produce clustered seedheads, greeny-brown, like a collection of tiny pebbles.

Habitat
Beside slow-running or stagnant water, often with roots totally submerged.

Height
Up to 105cm (42in).

Preparation
Cut when the seedheads are well formed, and hang upside down.

Alisma plantago–aquatica

ANGELICA SYLVESTRIS (angelica)

Wild or wood angelica is the wild cousin of the cultivated variety, the stems of which are used for candying and making the bright green cake decoration. Wild angelica has the same distinctive sweet smell.

Habitat
Moist, weedy or woodside places alongside water.

Height
50cm–2m (20in–7ft).

Preparation
Cut when the seedheads have formed, retaining as much stem as wished.

ARMERIA MARITIMA (thrift, common pink)

Tufts of rough short leaves produce round, pink, pompon flowers on straight bare stems.

Habitat
Sandy, seaside places, on sand dunes, or clinging to rocks, cliff faces, surviving on no visible nutrients.

Height
Up to 45cm (18in).

Preparation
Cut as soon as the flowers are just about to open out. Too late and they lose their colour fast when dry, turning a dull pinky grey. Hang to dry.

Chamaenerion angustifolium

CHAMAENERION ANGUSTIFOLIUM
(rosebay, willowherb, fireweed)

Brilliant deep or pale-pink flowered stalks can transform an area into a blaze of colour, hence one of its common names being 'fireweed'. Spectacular anywhere except one's own garden, where it will self-seed to epidemic proportions, and prove nearly impossible to eradicate. The seedheads and fluff surrounding them dry well.

Habitat
Edges of woodlands, deciduous, coniferous or mixed.

Height
Up to 1.4m (54in).

Preparation
Cut when the fluffy surrounding to the seedheads has formed and prop upright. Good for spraying with copper colours, and bunching, mixed with other wild grasses and seeds.

CHENOPODIUM FAMILY
(goosefoot, fat hen)

Spikes of green or greyish green, tightly packed flowers on one main stem. Not unlike the dock family. Many varieties of this species, mostly all of which dry well.

Habitat
Mainly on waste ground, but road verges, edges of fields as well.

Height
Up to 1m (3½ft), some only up to 35cm (1ft).

Preparation
When the tall green flowering spike is still tightly-packed and green, cut from base of the stem, strip off leaves and lower branches, if any, and hang upside down. Beware of the thousands of tiny black seeds that shower in all directions when the stem is dry.

CHRYSANTHEMUM VULGARE
(tansy)

(Although of the tanacetum family, this plant now comes under chrysanthemum.)
Strong-smelling, deeply serrated leaves with clusters of button yellow flowers. This plant was in use for centuries, in tansy cakes, and placed underneath (but not eaten) in apple pies, but it is too strong for today's taste.

Habitat
On rich moist soil, such as wasteland, embankments, edges of woods.

Height
Up to 1.2m (4ft).

Preparation
Cut when the flower heads are really well out, but if possible before any tinge of brown creeps in. Strip off the lower leaves and hang upside down.

Chrysanthemum vulgare

DICRANELLA HETEROMALLA (moss)

Almost all types of moss dry well. The small, rounded, young mosses, found on crevices in walls, have lovely shapes and retain their shape and colour when dried, but tend to become very hard and brittle if pronged with flower stems. They are ideal for laying on a flat arrangement and using as an edging. The looser ground mosses can be more easily teased out and moulded round foam to disguise it.

Preparation

Pick at any time of the year when still green and as dry as possible. Beware of the insects, slugs, beetles, etc. that have their homes underneath, and shake them out to find another hiding place before bringing the moss home. Some moss which is gathered from the ground will probably need to have weeds and even small stones extracted.

Use a flat knife, or something like a kitchen spatula, for easing moss off stones or ground in one piece, and, if possible, lay in a flat basket or garden trug until you get home.

Dry by laying flat on a wire cake-tray, for example, or a piece of chicken wire stretched over a wooden orange box. I once made a drying area for moss by making a rough type of net effect with wool over a cardboard box and it worked perfectly. The plastic nets in which bags of citrus fruits are sold are also ideal if opened out, stretched over a box and stapled or attached with drawing pins to the sides.

Moss does not need to be dried fast. Even if left in a moderately warm room it will dry out totally in a remarkably short time.

DIGITALIS (foxglove)

Foxgloves produce wonderful green seedheads that can be dried – sometimes with great success, sometimes with very disappointing results. They are worth trying for their wonderful curving shapes.

Habitat
Beside woodland, both deciduous and coniferous, in sandy soil.

Height
Up to 1.2m (4ft).

Preparation
Cut when the seedheads are still forming, trimming off the top flowers as they do not dry.

DIPSACUS (teasel)

Fascinating plant that produces rounded prickly cones of flowers, which start off the summer green, produce a purple band of flower, and then turn brown and stiff.

Habitat
Stony places, well drained, along paths and wasteland.

Height
Up to 1.2m (4ft).

Preparation
Cut when the flowering is over and the brown head has emerged. Cut off a length of stem (the challenge seems to be how to cut them without receiving substantial scratches) and hang upside down to dry, or prop upright.

ERICA (heathers and heaths)

Most heathers can be dried very successfully, although the 'bell' heathers, which emerge earlier than

Dipsacus pilosus

the other types and have larger, brighter, bell-like flowers do not dry well.

Habitat
Upland, peaty soil, open countryside.

Preparation
Cut when the flowers are just forming, and the lower ones have

just emerged. Strip off the lower leaves and hang in small bunches upside down. For another method (sticking into a potato) see under *Erica* in perennial section.

EUPHORBIA
(spurge)

There are many types of wild euphorbias, which generally grow in a fairly rich soil and are one of the commonest garden weeds. Like all euphorbias, their juice can cause a mild rash on skin exposed to sunlight. The brilliant green of their early leaves dries true to colour, although in the drying process they can tend to look rather shrivelled. Sun spurge dries well.

Habitat
Weedy places in gardens, fields, and wasteland where the soil is fairly rich.

Height
Up to 30cm (1ft).

Preparation
Cut when the leaves have just formed and hang upside down. Takes some time to dry, and although will reduce in bulk considerably and become shrunken, the green colour is as bright as when fresh. The round leaves will still have some movement and rustle in a breeze.

FICALES FAMILY
(ferns)

Any wild fern is useful for drying. There are many varieties with different shapes, sizes and habitats; these are indigenous to the area and prolific. Examples of species are: asplenium, adiantum, athyrium, dryopteris and

pteridophyta. Mostly all grow in damp places, but smaller ones can be found in walls and stony places.

Preparation
Cut from the base of the stem when just out, stripping off the lower leaves to leave a prong to insert into foam. Press.

FILIPENDULA ULMARIA
(meadowsweet)

Meadowsweet, with its strongly scented flowers, produces green seedheads which dry beautifully. They are equally attractive when brown.

Habitat
Prolific in damp ditches beside country roads; any soil, provided it is damp.

Height
Up to 2m (7ft).

Preparation
Cut when the green seedheads have just formed, or wait until they turn brown. Hang to dry. Do not usually need spraying for seed loss.

Filipendula ulmaria

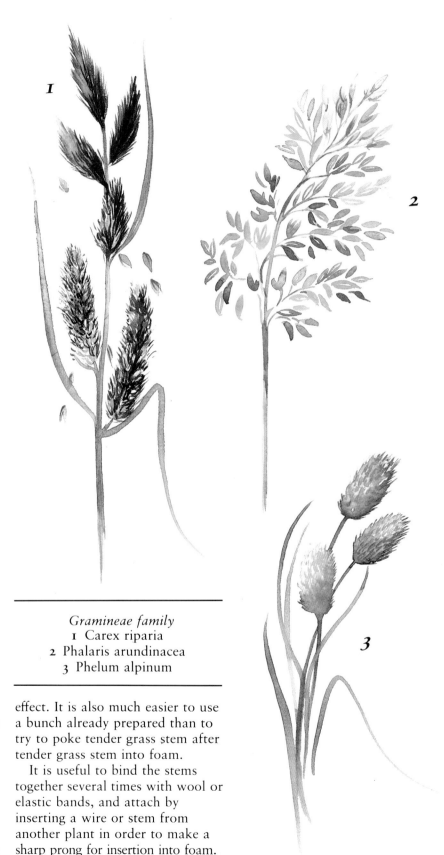

GALIUM VERUM
(ladies' bedstraw)

Low-growing plant, with yellow, straw-like flowers, which looks like a fine bottle brush. The common name is derived from the old practice of filling mattresses with the plant when in flower. Its slight springiness and honeyed scent no doubt added to its appeal.

Habitat
Dry turf, or sandy verges.

Height
Up to 60cm (2ft).

Preparation
Cut when the flowers are just forming, strip off lower leaves, and hang in tiny bunches.

GRAMINEAE FAMILY
(grasses)

Many grasses can be dried. Trial and error will be the guidelines for those indigenous to different areas. However, virtually all grasses should be cut early in the season after forming, hung upside down in small bunches by type and sprayed as soon as they are dried to stop massive seed dropping. Examples of grasses which can be dried and illustrated here include *Phalaris arundinacea* (canary grass), *Phleum alpinum* (cat's tail, alpine) *Carex riparia* (great pond sedge).

Grasses alone can make wonderful arrangements, as well as being sprayed gold and silver at Christmas.

Always take care to bunch grasses by type and ensure that they are the same trimmed length. Most grasses are far too fine to be used alone, and generally a bunch or so at a time needs to be used for

Gramineae family
1 Carex riparia
2 Phalaris arundinacea
3 Phelum alpinum

effect. It is also much easier to use a bunch already prepared than to try to poke tender grass stem after tender grass stem into foam.

It is useful to bind the stems together several times with wool or elastic bands, and attach by inserting a wire or stem from another plant in order to make a sharp prong for insertion into foam.

86

HERACLEUM SPHONDYLIUM
(cow parsnip, hogweed, keck)

Similar in appearance to angelica, with wide seedheads, but a less pleasant smell.

Habitat
Likes light soil, damp wood edges, meadows, woody places. Rabbits love it too, which may give a clue to its whereabouts!

Height
Up to 1.5m (5ft).

Preparation
Cut when the seedheads have formed, spray if necessary to stop seeds dropping and prop upright to dry.

KNAUTIA ARVENSIS
(scabious)

Attractive mauve/purple round flat flower that grows on tough stems.

Habitat
Dry turf and chalky soils. Edges of paths and fields.

Height
Up to 60cm (2ft).

Preparation
Cut when the tight little flower is still clamped shut, and the colour is that of pinky lavender. Dry by hanging.

LAPSANA COMMUNIS
(nipplewort)

Tiny, vivid yellow flowers top the stiff upright stems of this weed no one wants to have in their garden but usually does. When dry, the plant is almost identical to the fresh version, and a whole bundle of nipplewort placed in a vase against a white wall looks charming.

Habitat
Likes moist, rich soil, alongside vegetable fields, thickets, edges of woods.

Height
Up to 1.2m (4ft).

Preparation
Cut when the flowers are just out. Only a proportion are out at any one time, so cut on a good sunny day when the plant is still fairly young. When the flowers are over, the seedheads stay attractive and green. Hang upside down.

Knautia arvensis

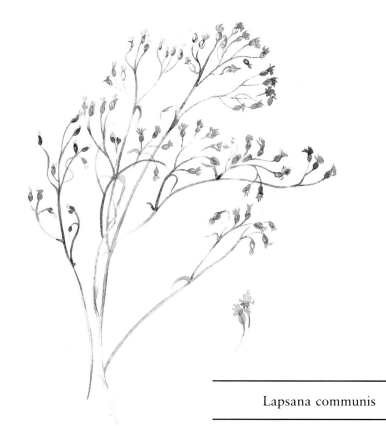

Lapsana communis

LEPIDIUM FAMILY
(pepperwort)

There are dozens of varieties of this common wild flower, which produces bright green fat flowers on a single stem, looking rather like a bottle brush. They dry well to retain their brilliant green colour.

Habitat
Waste places, edges of fields.

Height
Up to 50cm (20in).

Preparation
Cut when the stem has flat petalled flowers on the ends of fat, bright green stalks. Strip off lower leaves and hang upside down to dry.

MYRICA GALE
(bog myrtle)

Wild, hardy relative of the tender, cultivated variety. Dense, shrubby and aromatic, bog myrtle has tough, sharp woody stems and deciduous pointed, dark green leaves, which retain their evocative scent for some time. Ideal filler in arrangements.

Habitat
Northern areas, in ditches, anywhere marshy or where the roots can be kept constantly damp.

Height
Up to 60cm (24in).

Preparation
Cut during midsummer, when the leaves are well formed, but before they turn the very dark green of late summer. Cut from the base of the stem, or just trim off branches. Dry loosely propped upright in a container.

Phagmites communis

PHAGMITES COMMUNIS
(reeds)

These swaying silvery-green reeds grow by the banks of rivers, such as in Norfolk and on the Tay in Perthshire, and were traditionally used for thatching. The reeds have chocolate, feathery plumes tipped with purple and turn gold in the winter.

Habitat
River banks, lakes, and ponds.

Height
Up to 2.5m (8ft).

Preparation
Cut during the late spring or early summer when the deep-glowing plumes are at their best, or wait until the late autumn when the colour bleaches to gold. Hang upside down to dry.

POLYGONUM LAPATHIFOLIUM
(pale knotgrass)

Elongated, slim, sausage-shaped pink flowers dry very well, and the flower heads bunched together make the rather painstaking job of picking them worthwhile.

Habitat
In rich, moist soil, weedy places beside fields and close to, if not rooted in, slow-flowing water.

Height
Up to 60cm (24in).

Preparation
Cut when the flowers are not quite out, strip off leaves and hang upside down.

PTERIDIUM AQUILINUM
(bracken)

Introduced into the Highlands of Scotland bracken was rapidly spread by sheep, whose trailing coats dragged the seeds. Love it or hate it, the fresh green fronds press very well.

Habitat
All over the northern hemisphere on any hilly ground, uncultivated field; on loamy not peaty soil.

Height
Up to 1.2m (4ft).

Preparation
Cut when the leaves have just uncurled and formed. Cut from the base of the stem, or just cut off side branches. Press.

RUMEX ACETOSA
(sorrel)

A member of the dock family and a herb that produces long seedheads, often tinged with bright scarlet.

Habitat
Usually grows in all the same places as dock, and often alongside.

Height
Up to 90cm (3ft).

Preparation
Cut when the seedheads are tinged with red, or wait until the bronze colour appears, although by this time the stems often look rather sparse compared with dock and can be disappointing.

Rumex crispus

RUMEX CRISPUS OR OBTUSIFOLIUS
(docks)

Docks are wonderful for drying, either when bright green (a colour they retain well when dried), or when autumnal and coppery brown. Seeds rarely drop, which is a particular advantage.

Habitat
On wasteland, where it appears to grow with minimal nourishment, as well as on verges, woodland clearings. Prefers a drier soil.

Height
Up to 1.2m (4ft).

Preparation
Cut during midsummer when green, or wait until bronze. Chop at base of stem, strip off leaves, hang upside down. Spray if in any doubt of seeds dropping.

SANGUISORBA OFFICINALIS
(great burnet)

Very distinctive plant, not readily confused, which has small brown or deep purple egg-shaped small flowers, rough to the touch, on long thin stems. Very prolific when it occurs.

Habitat
Damp, peaty moorland, fens, damp meadows.

Height
Up to 1.5m (5ft).

Preparation
Cut when the flower balls have just coloured, or wait until they mature and turn brown. Hang upside down to dry.

SILENE VULGARIS
(bladder campion or white bottle)

Open white or pink flowers become fragile urn-shaped seedheads, white or cream with green or pink veining.

Habitat
Dry, open, sunny places, alongside paths.

Height
Up to 50cm (20in).

Preparation
Cut from the base of the stem, when the seedheads have just formed. As it is usually not possible to trim off the leaves without snapping off the stem, hang upside down in very small bunches to avoid rot in the stems.

Silene vulgaris

Trifolium medium

TRIFOLIUM MEDIUM
(clover)

Of the many varieties of clover, this one, the zig-zag, or meadow clover, does appear to dry best. The common name applies to the stem, with flower stalks zig-zagging from it. The pink, spherical flowers are easily spotted, as most other common clovers have far rounder flower heads.

Habitat
Turf, woodland edges, well drained soil.

Height
Up to 50cm (20in).

Preparation
Cut when the flowers are still tightly formed, and hang up to dry.

TYPHA ANGUSTIFOLIA
and *T. LATIFOLIA*
(reedmace, greater and lesser)

Towering stem is topped by a long brown oblong of smooth flower, with gold plume above.

Habitat
Edges of still fresh water, often found close to reeds.

Height
Up to 2.5m (8ft).

Preparation
Cut in the summer when the flower stem is fully formed, and prop upright to dry.

USNEA
(lichen)

Lichens dry well, and their greeny-grey colouring allies happily with most material.

Preparation
Pick all the year round, when dry. Lichen that has formed on a dead branch of silver birch, for example, could be removed with the outer bark. Can be scooped up with hands, but a spatula of some sort helps matters.

Vaccinium

Usnea

VACCINIUM MYRTILLUS, V.OXYCOCCUS, V.ULIGINOSUM, V.VITISIDAEA (*blueberry, bilberry, cranberry, whortleberry*)

Although all these are of a slightly different variety, they all grow on acidic soil, on twiggy, tough, branching, low growing stems and produce edible berries.

Habitat
Generally, where there is heather, there should be one of these growing.

Height
Up to 30cm (1ft).

Preparation
Cut from late autumn to early summer, when the leaves have more or less fallen off. The twigs are mostly attractive shades of green, and their strong stems make ideal props for other dried material. Prop upright and use directly in arrangements just after picking, as they will dry perfectly in foam, or hang upside down.

CULTIVATED VEGETABLES AND HERBS

ALLIUM PORRUM
(leek)

Left in the ground too late into spring, leeks will produce one round, pinkish flower shoot per plant.

Cultivation

They are a wonderful vegetable for eating, lengthy to mature and require much work and enriched soil, but there are always a few which do not thrive too well and are the last to be dug. Once the shoot is visible in the centre of the leek, it is in any case too tough to be edible. With a clear conscience, you can carefully transplant these in the spring to a corner of the garden and leave them to run to seed.

Preparation

Cut when the flower head is just formed, and is bursting out of its protective sheath. If you are too late in picking, the flower head becomes faded. Hang upside down in a place well away from other flowers, which can be impregnated with the oniony smell during the first few days of drying. If the head falls into a spherical shape, then prop upright to finish the drying process.

ALLIUM SCHOENOPRASUM
(chives)

Clumps of chives, which can be bought readily from most nurseries, produce round pink flower balls, which dry beautifully.

Allium porrum

Cultivation

Plant your clump in sun, or slight shade in medium-rich soil. Divide every four years and plant out about 30cm (1ft) apart.

Preparation

Cut as soon as the flowers have formed, chopping off from the base of the stem. Hang upside down.

ANGELICA ARCHANGELICA
(angelica)

Majestic biennial that grows easily from seed, obtainable from many seed merchants. Tender, early, slender stalks are used for candying for the green cake decorations, and when crushed, the plant has the distinctive sweet smell. A stalk placed in the bottom of a pan of rhubarb before cooking, but discarded before eating, counteracts any acidity.

Cultivation

Sow the seeds where you want them to flower, in a part of the garden where they can be left happily to self-seed, as this will continue indefinitely. The seeds are fairly heavy, so the spread will not be too great. An area of about 1.8 metres (6sq ft) should be adequate. Height up to 1.8 metres (6ft). Thin out to 35cm (15in).

Preparation

Cut when the circular seedheads, which first become green then turn brown, can be picked when well formed on a 30cm (1ft) stalk.

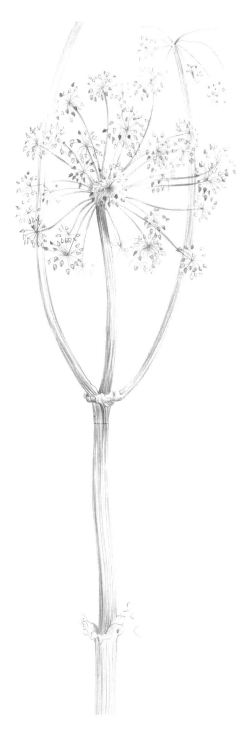

Alternatively, the entire stalk, cut off from just above ground level' can be dried. Prop upright. Benefits from being sprayed with gold for Christmas.

BETA VULGARIS CONDITIVA
(beetroot)

A surprising inclusion in this list, beetroot leaves can be press-dried with remarkable success, retaining their distinctive colouring, although with a slightly faded charm. They are rather paper-thin and fragile, and best used suspended by their stalk in arrangements.

Cultivation
Sow the seeds in early spring, thin out the rows to 30cm (1ft) apart. Plant in full sun, in fairly rich soil.

Preparation
Cut on a dry day when the leaves are well formed, and press. As the leaves are rather watery, they can take a long time to dry. If there has been a great deal of rain, it is not worth trying to gather them until three or four dry days have occurred.

CYNARA SCOLYMUS
(globe artichoke)

Globe artichokes can be grown easily from seed, obtainable from most seed merchants. They produce gracious, acanthus-like grey-silver leaves and an edible flower head.

Cultivation
Sow the seeds in summer for autumn transfer to permanent site, which should be sheltered and in fairly rich soil. Plant 75cm (30in) apart.

Preparation
Cut when the flower head is still tightly closed, or wait until the tufts of purple, thistly flower heads appear and pick immediately. If left too late the tufts can turn to thistledown and waft away. Prop upright in a jar or basket to dry.

Angelica archangelica

Beta vulgaris conditiva

DAUCUS CAROTA
(carrot)

Carrot leaves, with their feathery-green freshness' dry well. Almost all types of carrots produce suitable leaves.

Cultivation
Sow seeds in open sunny position, in soil that is unmanured, and fairly light. Thin out to 20cm (8in) or so apart.

Preparation
Cut when the carrots are harvested, and hang the leaves upside down or carefully open out and press.

FOENICULUM VULGARE
(fennel)

Both the annual, Florence fennel (F. v dulce), and the perennial, F. vulgare, produce waving aniseed-scented leaves that dry well, if picked young. The annual is easily grown from seed, obtainable from most seed merchants; the perennial can be grown from seed, but is usually available from herb nurseries.

Cultivation
Sow the annual seeds in a sunny position, ordinary garden soil in late spring. Plant the perennial in open, sunny ordinary ground.

Preparation
Cut as soon as the leaves, which reach a height of around 60cm (2ft), have formed, pick only a few from each plant. Hang upside down in the warmest part of the airing cupboard. The seedheads are often more successful to dry and they should be picked when fully mature, (i.e. the little seeds feel quite hard).

Foeniculum vulgare

HYSSOPUS OFFICINALIS
(hyssop)

Easily grown from seed, this aromatic perennial can be made into a low hedge, and if kept trimmed forms good bushy shapes. The bright, indigo blue flowers, which emerge in summer, can be picked for drying.

Cultivation
Sow the seeds in the summer, for planting out in the autumn. Plant 30cm (1ft) apart in ordinary soil, full sun.

Preparation
Cut as soon as the flower heads have fully formed and hang upside down.

Hyssopus officinalis

LAURUS NOBILIS
(bay)

Familiar to us through its culinary uses, bay can be dried by the stalk very well. Bay is tender anywhere, and in cooler climes should be grown in a pot and wintered in a cool place inside.

Cultivation
Can be grown from seed, but fairly easy to obtain as a plant. In a tub can be restricted to any size desired, often grown as a half or full standard.

Preparation
Cut during the summer when the leaves are at their glossiest, hang upside down, or press.

Lavendula spica

LAVANDULA SPICA
(lavender)

Probably the best known and loved of the herbs for drying. Aromatic, essential for pot pourri, lavender is also a moth-deterrent, can be steeped for an antiseptic, and a sprig will flavour sugar. Lavender is fairly easily grown from seed, obtainable from almost every seed merchant, as are small plants. Search for the unusual deep blue/purple colours as well as growing the gentle, pale types. Fairly short lived. Best propagated from cuttings.

Cultivation
Sow seeds in summer for planting out in the autumn in their permanent site, sunny position in ordinary, well drained soil. Plant 30cm (1ft) apart. Height up to 60cm (2ft). Trim down at the end of the season.

Preparation
Cut when the flower heads have just formed and are still tightly closed. Hang upside down.

MONARDA DIDYMA
(bergamot)

Perennial bergamot, which attracts bees and butterflies in profusion, produces flowers from scarlets to pale and brilliant magenta pinks. Although the flowers do shrivel a little, they retain their colour when dry. Seeds fairly easy to obtain from most seed merchants. Plants available from many nurseries, as well as herb specialists.

Cultivation
Sow seeds in summer for planting out in permanent site in the autumn, in groups of three or five; set 38cm (15in) apart. Eventual

RUTA GRAVEOLENS
(rue)

The strangely-scented blue-green ornamental leaves of rue can be pressed, but the bright yellow flowers are good value if picked for drying. Obtainable as plants from many nurseries, if not try herb nurseries.

Cultivation
Plant in ordinary soil, well drained and in full sun. Height up to 60cm (2ft); planting distance 45cm (18in).

Preparation
Cut when the flowers have just formed and hang to dry. Leaves picked in early summer can be pressed.

Origanum vulgare

height about 60cm (2ft). They need moist, rich soil. Occasionally suffer from mildew, which should be treated with proprietary spray.

Preparation
Cut when the flowers have just formed, and hang upside down.

ORIGANUM VULGARE
(marjoram)

Hardy perennial that can be grown very easily from seed, but equally easily bought as a plant.

Spreads happily. Produces deep pink-maroon flowers, which dry perfectly and retain their scent for several weeks after drying.

Cultivation
Plant in full sun, ordinary soil 30cm (1ft) apart; height the same.

Preparation
Cut when the flowers are fully formed, and use fresh for a herb wreath or herbal decoration, or hang upside down in small bunches to dry. The colour remains almost true to the fresh form.

Ruta graveolens

Salvia officinalis

SALVIA OFFICINALIS
(sage)

Both green and purple sage can be grown from seeds or plants, both of which can easily be obtained. The flower heads with their stiff bracts dry very well, and the leaves, if used fresh, form a very good base for herbal wreaths.

Cultivation
Plant in ordinary soil, sunny position, about 30cm (1ft) apart. Height up to 45cm (18in). The plants need firmly cutting down at the end of the season to keep their bushy shape.

ZEA MAYS
(sweetcorn or maize)

Both the ordinary yellow sweetcorn and the multi-coloured ornamental ones can be grown in Britain, provided there is a reasonable summer. More recent developments of seed give a greater assurance of success.

Cultivation
Sow the seeds under glass in the spring, and plant out in ordinary soil, sunny sheltered site. Plant 45cm (18in) apart, height up to 1.8cm (6ft). (I have planted these in the greenhouse to ensure ripening. They did ripen, but grew too tall and spent their last month bending over. However, in a wet summer, this at least produced a good crop.)

Preparation
Cut when the silky plumes appear at the end of the cob, the fruit is ripening, and should be ripe about four weeks or so later. The only way to test is to pull back the protecting leaves gently and see if the cobs have hardened and coloured. Ensuring that there are

Zea mays

only two cobs on each plant will mean each is uniform and near perfect.

Cut with a short stem, peel back the covering leaves and open them up slightly, leaving them to dry with the leaves forming a hammock effect round about. Hang the cobs from their stem to dry, or prop upright in a basket.

The male plume, which grows at the top of the plant, can be cut at end of the season and propped upright to dry.

OTHER FARM CROPS

Avena sativa

Hordeum vulgare

Triticum vulgare

AVENA SATIVA
(oats)

Can be picked when still green, and will dry very effectively at this stage in their development, retaining their colour indefinitely. Picked later when golden and ripe, they will retain their colour for several months, usually then fading to a golden blond tone.

HORDEUM VULGARE
(barley)

Can also be picked when green and the 'ears' stick straight upright. Later on, when the colour changes to gold and the heads bend over, they are just as beautiful.

TRITICUM VULGARE
(wheat)

Can be picked both when green and gold. The fat, golden heads when fully ripe look best in a bunch, the stalks trimmed to the same length.

ARRANGEMENTS

PREPARING MATERIAL

WIRING

Although some material does benefit from being wired, very few flowers really need to be. One notable exception is the helichrysum family, whose floppy heads will tend to fall over when dried, and then face downwards in arrangements.

Materials

Medium stub wire
The wires generally come in packets, ready-cut into convenient lengths of about 15–38cm (6–15in). Obtainable from florists.

Gutta-percha tape
Either use this direct from the reel, or, for ease and manageability, break off 15cm (6in) lengths, stick them temporarily to the table top, and use in sections. The tape is available in shades of creams and greens; a dull green suffices for almost everything.

Secateurs

Wire cutters

Wiring helichrysums

Method one
Pick only the flower heads off the stem as you progress along the rows. You need to wire them immediately because, when dry, they will become astonishingly hard and it will be impossible to insert even the sharpest wire.

Push the wire straight up through the stub of stem on the underside of the flower. When 2.5cm (1in) or so of wire is exposed, bend over the top, and gently pull it down again until the

hook you have made is concealed. Holding the gutta-percha tape at an angle, wind round the wire downwards for at least 15cm (6in), and conceal the wire.

Method two
Dry the flower heads with 7.5–10cm (3–4in) of stem still attached. Hold a wire to the stem, the top of the wire being just under the flower. Holding the gutta-percha tape at an angle, wrap it around both the stem and wire, not only binding them together, but also concealing the wire. Continue down for at least 15cm (6in).

Wiring helichrysums

You can then stick the wires into a block of foam to dry. They can be left like this for storing, or wrapped and stored in a box.

You can use them singly, or twist the wire stems together for an instant posy effect.

Wiring other materials
Other flowers are often picked with very short stems, and therefore need to be given a false wire stem which will not make them restricted to very low arrangements.

Among other materials which come into this category are:

Roses, if picked with short stems. As the stems are often so prickly, and therefore both sore on the hands and awkward for pushing into arrangements, where their thorns can often catch on other stems, it is an advantage to wire them.

Helipterum and *rhodanthe* have fine, fragile stems, and not only benefit from being given more secure stems, but also save much time by being grouped in small bunches.

Physalis alkekengi franchetii (Chinese lanterns) and *Nicandra physalodes* grow all the way down the stem, and the lower ones can be removed and given false stems of wire quite easily.

All these varieties can be wired in the same way, either when fresh or dried. Pick with a very short stem, hold the wire close to the stem in one hand, wrap round with gutta-percha tape, and continue winding down the wire until the whole wire is covered.

arrangements can produce the effect of a Seurat painting viewed too close.

To cheat a little, or to make a bunch of small flowers look as though they are one larger bloom, is effective and easy.

Small bunches of *Centaurea cyanus*, lonas, *Dianthus caryophyllus*, ammobium, polygonum, *Calendula officinalis*, gomphrena, *Alchemilla mollis*, santolina, armeria, etc. can be used in this way.

Bunch the flowers in your hand or on the table. Using a wire, bind round the stems just under the blooms, and continue down until all the stems are tied in. Disguise both stems and wire with gutta-percha tape.

You can use the same technique with larger flowers. The last of the season's *Achillea filipendulina* are often smaller than the ones flowering in the summer, and several smaller ones will make one that will match in size one larger bloom.

ADJUSTING
To add height
Sometimes the stems on some dried material are not tall enough for the arrangement. The easiest way to lengthen a stem is to attach it to another dried stem with gutta-percha tape. Spare dried stems of achilleas, aconitum, and delphiniums, where the flowers have been chopped off and used on shorter stems, are ideal as they dry very straight and strong.

Using wire to extend stem length is an excellent alternative if you want to be able to bend the stem at a different angle.

To make bunches
Dried flowers are often so small that unless you use several together in a bunch within an arrangement, the effect can be messy or insignificant. Using the smaller flower heads individually in largish

Bunch short-stemmed polygonums onto a natural stem with wire

A classic hall with a white and black floor is brightened up with this golden arrangement of physalis, white helichrysum, Centaurea macrocephala, Alchemilla mollis, *hydrangea*, Carthamus tinctorius, *solidaster, and chenopodium.*

SPRAYING

Light hair lacquers are essential to ensure that seedheads and some flower heads do not scatter their seeds.

Gather a collection of car spray paints for enhancing some materials. Many leaves benefit from a matching gloss of spray, or take on new dimensions with gold and silver for Christmas. For example:

- copper tones enhance docks and beech;
- blues and mauves give back colour to fading hydrangea heads;
- clear varnish gives extra lustre to nicandra seedheads and cones, and
- various shades of jades and emerald greens can be used on grey lichen; greens a shade deeper than fading moss will revive the colour for another few months.

Remember to choose the least-harmful sprays, and to use them sparingly in a well-ventilated room, or outside.

STEAMING

You can use the steam from a boiling kettle for branches and ferns in order to give material a more relaxed look.

Examples of material which can be freshened up by this method include:

- moss which has been crushed in storage;
- leaves which have been hung upside down and have therefore folded in on the stem too much;
- barley which has straightened out instead of curving over;
- flower petals on roses which have become folded under
- ferns which have shrivelled, and
- the parchment-type leaves surrounding sweetcorn which have dried too stiffly.

Hold the piece by the stem over a kettle which is kept on the boil, and allow the steam to penetrate the material thoroughly (this will take from 30 to 60 seconds). Removing the leaf from the steam, gently stroke it with fingers until it straightens out, or, in the case of moss, tease it with fingers, a fork, or a skewer until it fluffs up. Some leaves, such as holly or oak, can benefit from stroking with fingers

Small flowers are snipped and bunched together on wire and then taped

which have just been smeared with a tiny drop of cooking oil.

In the case of sweetcorn, the stiff leaves which might have been intended to dry with a cradle-effect round the cob, but have stiffened too much in the drying process, can be steamed one at a time, and opened up to re-form an attractive fan-shaped frame.

Allow everything to dry thoroughly again if re-storing. If steaming just prior to arranging, then most material will dry naturally in an arrangement.

This flat pink Filpino basket is decorated with pink annual delphinium (larkspur), pinky-green hydrangea florets, bought dyed moss, pale pink helichrysum and gypsophila.

ARRANGING

When all the flowers are dried and stacked, hung, or packed, you should be looking at a much larger collection than you thought you could grow, collect, and dry. The next stage is to arrange them, and many people feel equally mystified about where to start arranging as they did about deciding what to dry.

Where do you begin? Don't be discouraged, or get into the habit of leaving them, as one friend has done for years, hanging where they dried from the kitchen ceiling. Although a ceiling swathed in flowers looks lovely, the rest of the house appears a trifle bare.

Ideally you should arrange in a room with good light, and as little draught as possible, as some dried flowers are as light as thistledown and can float away. Therefore, try to avoid any main thoroughfares in your house, and choose instead somewhere you can be undisturbed for a day or so. Dried flowers make a substantial mess, and, once having begun on arranging, it's better for your sanity to keep going until you have finished, then sweep up the debris. I find any way of minimizing the endless clearing up of mess a bonus. (It is useful to have a smooth floor from which the trimmings can be swept up easily.)

MATERIALS

- An old table, or one that can be well-protected with an oilskin, chopping board, etc.
- Secateurs
- Florists' wire
- Wire cutters
- The special grey foam obtainable from florists' shops in various shapes (start off with the large oblong blocks)
- Large kitchen knife for cutting up the foam
- Pair of sharp kitchen scissors
- Container, if being used
- Florists' spike (with a sharp prong on top and a suction pad underneath)

BEFORE YOU BEGIN

1. First of all, look around the house and decide where you want an arrangement to be placed. Decide whether it should be: on a table, to be viewed either from above or at eye-level; hanging from the wall, for example in a basket, or on top of a tall chest, to be viewed from below.

2. Look at the background. Avoid somewhere with daylight permanently shining through, as even the most substantial arrangement can look sparse. Is the background to be a plain wall, patterned or plain curtains; will there be ornaments? Study the surrounding colours.

3. Choose a container. It can be virtually anything, from baskets, to small wooden boxes, glass, or china vases, pottery plant-pots, brass, copper, or silver, etc. Broken, chipped or leaking containers are fine for dried material. Make sure that you weight down the container with pebbles, sand, etc.

Clear glass containers
If you want to use a clear glass container, you might find that the stalks look somewhat unattractive. To disguise them, place a block of foam into the vase, securing it well by tying it down, or using florists' spikes.

Round the foam you can pour any, or a combination, of the following: pot pourri; small shells; clean, very dry sand (baked in the oven); dried flower heads, or small broken pieces of flower; moss; dried beans, e.g. lentils, kidney beans, mung beans, etc., or a mixture of several types; dried pasta; dried herbs, or even tea, especially the type mixed with dried jasmine flowers.

4. Place the chosen container on the spot. Have a good look at it.

5. Bring along a few flowers and hold them up, experimenting with the colours. Nature provides few colours which clash, but for beginners, it may be as well to stick to a restricted number to start with. (See colour coordination on p. 99)

7. Keep a sense of proportion about all this! Remember that a bunch of flowers, even if all the same type, will look better in a suitable container than will an over-ambitious scheme. Large flowers need large containers, and plenty of room in which to display them. A hydrangea head will look fairly ridiculous in a sugar bowl, and, conversely, a few grasses and the odd selection of *Centaurea cyanus* and Ionas will be lost in a china bowl the size of a bucket.

8. If it is at all possible to do the arrangement where it is finally to

Formal cut-glass vase filled up with pot pourri and arranged with blue perennial delphinium, deep red Paeonia lactiflora, deep pink Polygonum bistorta 'Darjeeling red' (knotgrass), grey Stachys lanata 'Cotton boll' (lamb's tongue), pink-blue hydrangea heads, blue Eryngium alpinum, gypsophila and lepidium.

sit, then do this. Most of the time it is not, so set up the container where you are going to do the arrangement.

POINTS TO REMEMBER

1. Make one or two arrangements using a generous amount of flowers, rather than try to spread the flowers around into many posies.

2. Try to chose a spot where the posy will be viewed mostly from one position, rather than where it will be seen from every angle.

3. Choose the easiest of the following suggestions, and, as you gain confidence, you can progress.

ARRANGING WITH FOAM
A basic arrangement
Most arrangements use a container filled mainly with greenery, and a few flowers. If possible, set up the container at the same height from which it will eventually be viewed. Fill up the container with foam.

Using the kitchen knife, estimate the size needed by standing the container on the foam, and cutting round it. Tighten up loose corners by infilling with slivers of foam. Make sure that the foam is really secure inside the container and will not wobble or move. Make sure that the level of the foam is just below the level of the container.

If you think that the foam might eventually show, then now is the time to cover it up with moss. Just place teased-out moss on the foam; there is no need to fix it, as it will be impaled by the stems of flowers, etc.

With the container facing you, place greenery, grasses, etc. in a fan

A large arrangement using a blue colour scheme to complement the décor. White helichrysum, lepidum, delphinium, hydrangea, Papaver somniferum *(poppy), white larkspur, and* Stachys lanata *(lamb's tongue) are used.*

shape at the back. A general rule is that the height of the tallest item should be twice the height of the container. Use the tallest and largest material for the background, and the smaller and shorter as you progress forwards to the front. You can use a wide variety of greenery, or just one type. (To make sure that you fill in in decreasing order of height towards the front, it might help to turn the container sideways and fill in one half, then turn it around and fill in the other.) Check that the whole area is covered. You should now have a container that is well filled with greenery.

Turn it around to face you, and start placing in the flowers. (Odd numbers of flowers – 3, 5, 7 – look better than even numbers for some reason.) Bunch the flowers and place several close together rather than dotting them around. Add one type and one colour at a time, and keep on adding until you feel you cannot squeeze in any more. Admire your masterpiece!

On a flat plate, tray, or basket
This is a very good way of using up the many flower and seedheads left over or broken off at the end of an arranging session. The idea of filling up a plate with dried flowers instead of food appeals to my sense of humour. You can fill a pretty tea cup with flowers and give it away with a saucer as a present.

Unexpected flattish containers filled with flowers also bring a smile. Give a keen cook a flower-filled cake tin, jelly mould, or small fancy pastry tin, preferably with the flowers on a foil tray so that she can actually use the tin. A passionate gardener could have a trowel filled with flowers.

If possible, wedge foam into the centre of a tray. With smooth plates, etc., use a florists' spike to secure the foam to the plate.

Another possibility is to wind thread, wool, or fine wire over the top and underneath to hold the foam in place. This can easily be made invisible by using raffia round baskets, narrow shiny Christmassy ribbon in the appropriate colour round silver, brass, copper, or gold, and thin florists' wire round glass, etc. Next, cover the foam with moss.

Flattish containers lend

themselves well to symmetrical shapes (for example, diamond shapes are fairly easy to do), and you need not be too ambitious; although I do remember seeing one heroic copy of a Persian carpet, which was a magnificent idea that on closer inspection was possibly within the capabilities of most.

Try to have some sort of a plan in mind; for example, start by dotting the palest colours/seedheads/small pieces of greenery until there is a definite background created, then use the brighter flower heads last.

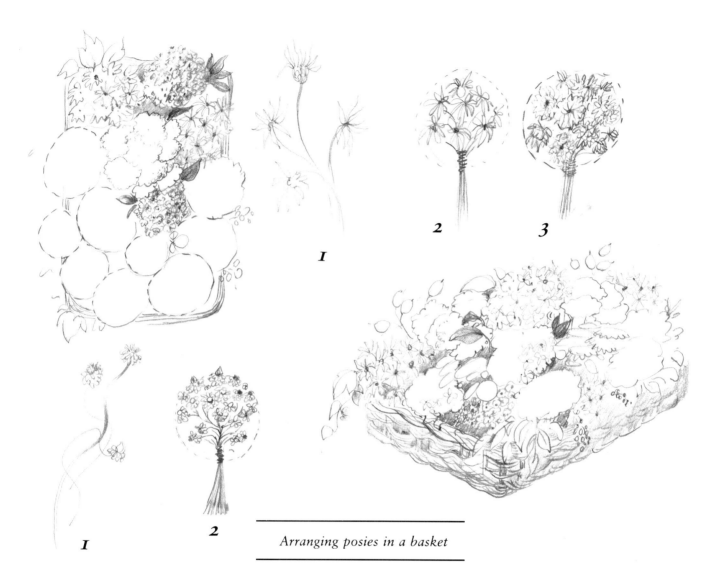

Arranging posies in a basket

Using almost entirely flower and seedheads on very short stems, stick in the material until almost the entire surface is covered.

The beauty of this quick and effective method is that, should you want to change your mind, you can quite easily pull everything out and do it again.

ARRANGING WITHOUT USING FOAM

This very easy way of arranging uses a low-rimmed container (such as a basket), no foam, and several types of flowers of similar size, either individually or in posies.

Assemble as many bunches as you can of, for example, lonas, lavendula, xeranthemums, *Centaurea cyanus*, gnaphalium, ammobium, which you have already dried as posies, and which are all roughly the same size and vary little in height. Most should have stems of little more than the depth of the container.

If they are not already prepared in this way, bunch together small posies of flowers, by separate type, so that they end up all about the same size. Trim all the stems so that they are roughly the same length per posy.

Starting from the outside edge of the basket, fill in with small ready-made posies. You can use all different colours (for instance, pinks, yellows, white and blues look very summery), or just two or three types in rings, which is equally effective. Ring the edge with pink rhodanthe, then fill in with dark lavender, and make a central circle with paler lavender.

1

2

3

4

Filling a basket

An eye-catching Christmas table arrangement, with Carlina acaulis, *green reindeer moss, red roses,* Achillea ptarmica, *and gypsophila. Red lacquered baskets add the final touch.*

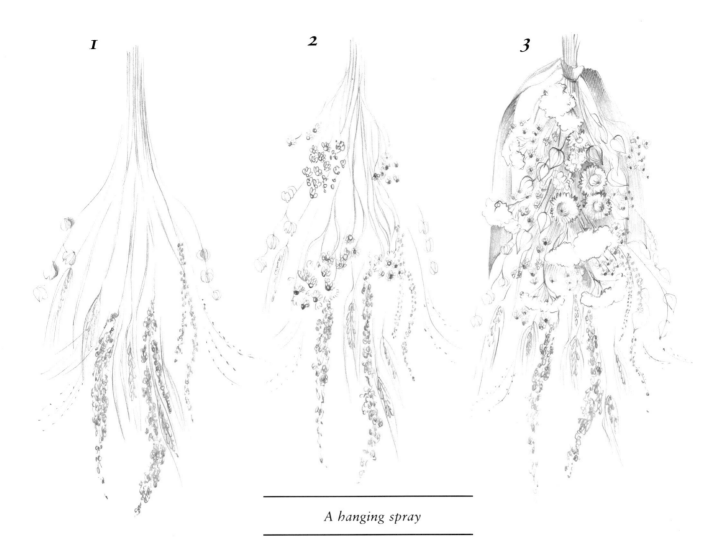

1

2

3

A hanging spray

HANGING BUNCHES

Choose where you want to hang your bunch, and decide what height. It is effective to make two matching bunches.

On a table or the floor, lay out the background of the longest, flattest material you have. Measure out the length, and, if necessary, elongate the stems with more stem or wire (see notes on wiring and adjusting on pp. 100–101). Then lay on top more and more material, becoming smaller in scale and length. If necessary, hold the top of the bunch in case some tries

to roll off. Place the smallest flowers on top.

The sequence of flower types could be as follows:

Lowest, longest material – rumex (docks), filicales (ferns), pteridium (bracken), *Fagus sylvatica* 'Cuprea' (copper beech), hedera (ivy), *Delphinium consolida* (larkspur).

Second layer (contrasting colours and material) – gramineae (grasses), hordeum (barley), triticum (wheat), astilbe, lunaria (honesty).

Third layer – wired helichrysums, the heads of which can be bent forwards to lie flat, achillea, *Alchemilla mollis*, anaphalis, astrantia, gnaphalium.

Top layer – small items, such as rosa (roses), helipterum, armeria.

Holding the top of the bunch in one hand, secure the stems together with a length of either wire, string, or wool, or a large elastic band. (I find the latter the easiest.)

Take the bunch to the place where it is eventually to hang, and

A pink colour scheme

A blue colour scheme

try it for effect. When you are satisfied, trim off the uneven lengths of stem. Make sure that you then make a very secure wire or string loop from which to hang it. Disguise the tie with a bow of ribbon, raffia, or winding round it with a flexible leaf or fern.

To make a pair of hanging bunches, prepare them side by side, adding the same layers.

USING STIFF MATERIAL AS A PROP

You can use large items of stiff, dried material as an arrangement in their own right and as a prop for other smaller items. Some suggestions are given below.

A large bunch of gypsophila can be secured into a slim-necked container, and then small flower heads propped amongst the stems or even smeared lightly with ordinary glue and stuck in place. Tiny white heads of anaphalis, white helichrysum and ammobium are wonderful and give a lovely airy look. *Sarothamnus scoparius* (Broom) is so spiky that many things can be securely embedded in it. You could dry a bird's nest and place it in the middle.

Whole larix (larch) branches can be dried and decorated with ammobium flowers, stuck on with glue. Ideally, a hot glue gun makes this surprisingly easy even for absolute beginners, although it can be time-consuming.

Whole young trees, such as manageable-sized *Betula pendula* (silver birch), larix (larch), or large branches of gnarled *Malus sylvestris* (apple) or *Pyrus communis* (pear) can be decorated with flower heads of, for example, physalis, stuck on with glue. You

An arrangement of lepidium, hydrangea, pink helichrysum, delphinium, aconitum, achillea and anaphalis.

will have to cut down the trees in the autumn and allow them to hang upside down and dry. Any leaves which still cling on can usually be shaken off quite easily.

ARRANGING WITHOUT USING CONTAINERS

Dried flowers can be tucked on top of wardrobes, dressers, and mantlepieces, as well as around mirrors, pictures, clocks, plates, and ornaments. Flowers used at a height that is well above eye level provide an ideal way of using up less than perfect material.

Using material in this way generally always means doing the arrangement *in situ*, so shroud the area in dustsheets first. Have a plan in mind regarding type and colour of flowers to use, and if you keep this simple, you will find that the leftovers and trimmings will be minimal.

Wardrobes, dressers, mantlepieces
Start by wedging the foam where you want it to go; fix it in place by either: inserting panel pins or drawing pins discreetly, and using them to zig-zag thread across the foam, or using several florists' spikes, if necessary held onto the surface by children's modelling material.

Mirrors, pictures, plates, clocks
If a mirror or picture is hanging from a wire, as opposed to being screwed to the wall, it is fairly easy just to wedge the foam in behind. As the mirror or picture will probably not be moved too much, this should be secure enough. If you think that the foam will show, cover it up with teased-out moss.

An arrangement above a grandfather clock

Wreath made from twists of leafless Betula pendula *(birch) twigs wired with green hydrangea, annual linum seedpods (flax), terracotta helichrysum, blue annual delphinium and bought dyed moss.*

A *festive wreath made from birch branches, hydrangea,* Eryngium
planum, *reindeer moss and red helichrysum, decorated with a tartan
ribbon.*

Using long pieces of material, such as bamboo, reeds, ferns, grasses, etc., make a 'frame' for the arrangement. Then fill in with other material, leaving the brightest colours to the end, and therefore the front.

Left-over pieces of material, such as flower heads that have lost their stalks, can be glued directly onto frames, or used round basket handles in arrangements.

N.B. You can also use ivy, hops, etc. – anything that 'drapes' over mirrors or pictures – gently kept in place with drawing pins.

An arrangement nestling above a mirror

WREATHS AND RINGS

These can be bought ready-made, but practice soon produces results. One way to arrive at the desired circle for a ring shape is to cheat a little and base the shape on a ready-bought round wire. Wreath shapes can be bought from florists (sometimes) but the easiest way is to buy lampshade framing.

The lampshade rings used to make stiff shades are ideal, and come in a wide variety of sizes. They are made from a wire strong enough to withstand the weight and tugging of considerable numbers of stems, etc. Old lampshades are often available at jumble sales, junk shops, etc., and you can very neatly cut off the outer rings with wire cutters and discard the rest.

To make a wreath using stems of vitis (vine), lonicera (honeysuckle), betula (birch), clematis, etc., you should try to work with fresh material. Pick in the very late autumn or winter, when all the leaves have fallen off; the stems will then twine and bend more easily, and dry once in place.

Twine the stems round the wire, attaching with small lengths of florists' wire, until the original wire base is totally concealed. Small items of dried material can then be inserted, and held in place, if loose, with small pieces of wire.

Fresh herbs cut into smallish lengths can be placed directly onto

the wire base and attached with small wires. The idea is to go round and round the wire, covering up the previous stems and wires with the flower heads of the next bunch.

It's an ideal job to do in the summer sitting out in the garden. You can use it as the ultimate excuse for sitting down on a hot summer's day, which is when herbs are best picked for drying. Of course, herb wreaths are practical too, as they were intended for use in the kitchen.

You can use several of these rings, in different sizes, attached together, as in the Olympic sign. This is one way of making a large arrangement on a wall, using minimal material.

Covered hoops

An Easter wreath made from birch branches, hydrangea, linum, and abandoned bird's nests. Chocolate eggs could also be used.

Heart-shaped wreath, wired with tiny bunches of pink roses, 'Golden salmon superieur' and 'Paul Crampel' and white gypsophila.

Wreath made from twists of leafless Betulas pendula (birch) twigs wired with green hydrangea, annual linum seedpods (flax), terracotta helichrysum, blue annual delphinium and bought dyed moss.

SUPPLIERS IN BRITAIN

Most local nurseries should stock almost all of the plants which are listed in this book. However, here are some useful contacts.

GENERAL HERBACEOUS PLANTS

Delphiniums
Blackmore and Langden
Pensford
Nr Bristol
BS18 4JL

Beth Chatto's Unusual Plants
Elmstead Market
Colchester
CO7 7DB

General
Wallace and Barr
Marden
Kent
TN12 9BP

BULBS

Broadleigh Gardens
Dept. G
Bishops Hill
Taunton
TA4 1AE

Potterton and Martin
The Cottage Nursery
Moortown Road
Nettleton
Caistor
Lincolnshire
LN7 6HX

CLEMATIS

John Beach
9 Grange Gardens
Wellesbourne
Warwick

Caddick's
10 Richmond Avenue
Grappenhall
Warrington
Cheshire
WA4 2ND

FERNS

Fibrex
Honeybourne Road
Pebworth
Nr Stratford-upon-Avon
CV37 8XT

J. K. Marston
Culag
Green Lane
Nafferton
Driffield
East Yorks

HEATHERS

The Heather Garden
139 Swinston Hill Road
Dinnington
S31 7RY

Pennyacre Nurseries
Dept GNO
Station Road
Springfield
Fife
KY15 5RU

HERBS

Scotherbs
Waterybutts
Grange
By Errol
Perthshire
PH2 7SZ

Wells and Winter
Mereworth
Maidstone
Kent
ME18 5NB

IVY

Fibrex
Honeybourne Road
Pebworth
Nr Stratford-upon-Avon
CV37 8XT

ROSES

David Austin
Bowling Green Lane
Albrighton
Wolverhampton
WV7 3HB

Peter Beales
Attleborough
Norfolk
NR17 1AY

Cocker's
Whitemyres
Lang Stracht
Aberdeen
AB9 2XH

Mattocks
Nuneham Courtenay
Oxford
OX9 9PY

SEEDS

Chiltern Seeds
Bortree Stile
Ulverston
Cumbria
LA12 7PB

Thompson and Morgan
London Road
Ipswich
IP2 0BA

SEED MERCHANTS IN THE USA AND CANADA

GENERAL MERCHANTS OF FLOWER AND VEGETABLE SEEDS

Alberta Nurseries and Seeds
Bowden
Alberta
Canada
TOM OKO

Archias' Seed Stores
PO Box 109
Sedalia
MO 65301

Earl May Seed and Nursery
PO Box 500
Shenandoah
IA 51603

Fisher's Seeds
PO Box 236
Belgrade
MT 59714
(*For high altitudes and short growing seasons*)

J. L. Hudson
PO Box 1058
Redwood City
CA 94064
(*Also called 'World Seed Service', rare plants from around the world*)

Landreth's Seeds
180 West Ostend Street
Baltimore
MD 21230
(*Apparently the oldest seed company in the USA*)

Park Seed Co.
PO Box 46
Greenwood
SC 29648
(*Also large herb section*)

Talavaya
PO Box 707
Santa Cruz Station
Santa Cruz
NM 87507
(*Native American southwest seeds for dry climates*)

REGIONAL SPECIALISTS (USA)

North east
Allen
Sterling and Lothrop
101 US Route 1
Falmouth
ME 04105

Comstock
Ferre and Co.
PO Box 125
Wethersfield
CT 06109

Golden Acres Farm
RR 2
Box 7430
Western Avenue
Fairfield
ME 04937

Mid-Atlantic region
Southern Exposure Seed
    Exchange
PO Box 158
North Garden
VA 22959

South east
Hastings
PO Box 4274
Atlanta
GA 30302

Wyatt Quaries Seed Co.
PO Box 739
Garner
NC 27529

Florida
Kilgore Seed Co.
1400 W. First Street
Sanford
FL 32772

Rocky Mountains
Mountain Seed and Nursery
PO Box 9107
Moscow
ID 83843

North west
Tillinghast Seed
PO Box 738
LaConner
WA 98257

California
California Gardeners Seed Co
904 Silver Spur Suite 414
Rolling Hills Estates
CA 90274

Lockhart Seeds
PO Box 1361
Stockton
CA 95205

South west
Aurora Garden
321 Texas Blvd
Texarkana
TX 75501

INDEX OF PLANTS BY LATIN AND COMMON NAMES

Bold figures refer to pages on which illustrations appear